THE NATURE OF
CREATIVE ACTIVITY

THE NATURE OF
CREATIVE ACTIVITY

Experimental and Comparative Studies of
Visual and Non-Visual Sources of Drawing,
Painting, and Sculpture by means of the
Artistic Products of Weak Sighted and
Blind Subjects and of the Art of Different
Epochs and Cultures

By

VIKTOR   LOWENFELD

ROUTLEDGE & KEGAN PAUL LTD
BROADWAY HOUSE, CARTER LANE
LONDON, E.C.4
Republished 1976
Scholarly Press, Inc., 22929 Industrial Drive East
St. Clair Shores, Michigan 48080

First published in England 1939
Second edition 1952
Reprinted 1959
Translated from the German by

O. A. OESER

LC 76-44934
ISBN 403-07211-5

CONTENTS

CONTENTS

INDEX OF FIGURES AND PLATES

The first column gives the number of the figure, the second and third columns the age of the pupil in years and months when the drawing was made. The fourth column gives his initials, and details about the pupils' sight defects can be found in Table II on page 16.

A. FIGURES

B. PLATES

Unless otherwise indicated all photographs are by the author.

The first column gives the number of the Plate, the second column the age of the pupil. The third column gives the pupils' initials, and details of their sight defects will be found in Table I, p. 15. Where no initials are given the drawing is by a normal sighted subject.

PLATE

	Yrs.	Mths.		
1.	13			"Moses Strikes the Rock That Water May Flow." Normal sighted; visual type.
2.	13.			As above. Haptic type.
3.	13.			"Jacob's Dream." Normal sighted; visual type.
4.	13.			As above. Haptic type.
5a.	12.		Sch. G.	"Drowning Man."
5b.	16.		M. B.	Drowning Man. (Detail from " Egyptians drowning in the Red Sea.")
6.	13.			"The Deluge." Normal sighted; haptic type.
7.	13.			"Moses Breaks the Tablets." Normal sighted; haptic type.
8.	23.		J M.	"Being Throttled." The powerful sensations concentrated in the eyes are represented by much exaggerated bulging eyeballs. Weak sighted; haptic type.
9.	18.		(Blind)	"Longing For Sight." Congenitally blind; visual type.
10a.	13.		S. Gr.	"Street."
10b.	13.		S. Gr.	"School on Fire."
11.	14.		S. Gr.	"Sleighs."
12.	14.		S. Gr.	"Skaters on the Ice." (In colours.)
13a.	15.		M. B.	"Forest under Snow and Woman Gathering Wood."
13b.	13.		S. Gr.	"Forest under Snow and Woman Gathering Wood."
14a.	12.		Sch. G.	Spray of Flowers, drawn from nature.
14b.	12.		Sch. G.	Spray of Flowers, drawn from memory.
15.	18; to 18;	4. 10.	M. M.	Developmental Series characteristic of the visual type. (1) Proletarian Woman, (2) Angry Man, (3) Screaming Man, (4) Exalted Woman, (5) Fanatical Orator.
16.	15; to 16;	4. 0.	H. A.	Developmental Series characteristic of the haptic type.
17.	15;	4.	H. A.	"Drowning Man."
18.	15;	5.	H. A.	"Laughing Man."
19.	15;	6.	H. A.	"Angry Man."
20.	16;	0.	H. A.	"Beggar."
21.	15;	7.	H. A.	"The Cry For Help."
22.	15;	9.	H. A.	Incomplete drawing. This is an intermediate stage of the mask "Man Trembling with Fear ", Pl. 23.
23.	15;	9.	H. A.	"Man Quivering with Fright." (In colours.)
24.	15;	9.	H. A.	"A Father Hears of the Death of His Son."
25.	15;	11.	H. A.	"Exhausted Proletarian Woman."
26.	16;	0.	H. A.	"Chess Player."
27.	17;	0.	S. Gr.	"Sunset." (In colours.)
28.	18;	0.	G. St.	"Angry Man."

PREFACE

Between those who can see and those who are blind
there are cases whose sight is not adequate for visual
perception yet whose 'blindness' is disturbed because
they are not entirely without light. These are the weak
sighted and they are psychologically the most difficult
to assess. In this book an attempt is made to investigate
the psychological basis of their creative activity. By making
an analysis of the artistic work of the weak sighted it may
be possible to make an approach to the phenomena on the
threshold between seeing and not seeing and so to achieve
the separation of visual from non-visual experiences.

The book is divided into three main parts. The first
section is concerned with an examination of the drawings
of children which are analysed from the first stroke up to
the point at which a conscious perception of space and form
is achieved. An inquiry is made into the experiences in
which the work has its origin and the drawings are classified
according to the type of experience they portray. In the
second part the author examines and analyses in detail
the more developed artistic work of the weak sighted and
displays the types of talent which in their purest form have
led him to distinguish two creative types. The third part is
intended to establish the general validity of the facts covered
in this specialised field. These results are compared with
the artistic output of normal sighted people and it is shown
that numerous parallels can be drawn to the forms of art
of widely different epochs and places.

The material for these investigations is the work of many
thousands of children and more mature people and is the
product of my teaching of the weak sighted and blind in
Vienna at the Hohe Warte Institute for the Blind, directed
by Siegfried Altmann. For about fifteen years I have been
intensively concerned with the artistic problems of the blind
and those of weak sight and for the same period have taught

normal people. In addition, I have myself been deeply interested in the general problems of art. Consequently, I have had the opportunity not only of studying the genesis of thousands of works but also of making those comparative studies whose outcome is to be found in this book.

Ten years ago I came into contact with Dr. Ludwig Münz, and it was due to him that the theoretical foundations for research into the plastic work of the blind were laid. He paid particular attention to the work of those born blind, and it was this that made it possible to find a better foundation than hitherto for further research. Under his suggestion, too, were instituted those developmental series which show that often just those pieces which appear to have little æsthetic appeal enable us, when they are placed in their context, to comprehend the growth or development of form and space conceptions in the blind.

It was in *Die Plastischen Arbeiten Blinder*, particularly in the second part where he defines the common basis of the formal and spatial conceptions of the blind and of the seeing and with it their relative capacity for the articulation of these conceptions, that provided in many essential points the theoretical premises for my scientific work. His penetrating analysis of the plastic work of the blind stressed for the first time the importance of such subjects as the articulation of representative signs, the overemphasis of significant details, muscular modes of perception, autoplastic experience of form, the symbolic representation of space and time, the affective articulation of space, and the form and space conceptions of the blind. Münz shows that these laws of formal comprehension hold good equally for the blind and the seeing, and thus on many decisive points his work provides a new foundation for research on modes of expression in artistic activity generally.

At the end of this preface I feel compelled to indicate humbly that as an artist and painter I myself have felt the creative forces of the unconscious and super conscious. I have experienced the throes of creative activity and have often, after a hard fight, had to admit failure. So, seen from another standpoint, this book sometimes appears to me as an act of self-immolation, which, although it may be cruel to oneself, may, I hope, bring many truths and much insight to the service of science and art.

I should like to place on record my indebtedness to Mr. Siegfried Altmann, Director of the Vienna Institute for the Blind, who allowed me complete freedom in organising the teaching and thus gave the necessary scope to these researches. My thanks are also due to Dr. Oeser for his excellent and lucid translation ; and to Mr. Carl Ehrenstein, who in numerous ways assisted in the completion of the work.

The medical details on p. 16 have been taken with the Director's permission from the records of the Institute. Professor E. Singer and Miss Rosa Büchler very kindly assisted in providing comparative material from the lowest age groups.

Most especially am I grateful to Dr. Anna Adler, who took a continuous and personal interest in the work.

VIKTOR LOWENFELD.

VIENNA.
September, 1938.

PREFACE
TO THE SECOND EDITION

Since the first edition of this book was published much work has been done which either directly or indirectly has some bearing on our problem. We can divide these activities into three categories :

(1) Research, and applications of it, which deals with the *educational implications* of the investigation with which this book is concerned.

(2) *Psychological implications* of the two creative types evolving out of the analysis of the creative work reported in this publication.

(3) Discussions on the *aesthetic implications* which deal with the problem of visual and haptical experiences of shape and form in general.

Educational Implications : Most outstanding of all research and publications which deal with the problem of creative types—in particular in regard to child art—is *Education through Art*, by Herbert Read.[1] In it Herbert Read strongly elaborated on one of my findings " that even the earliest schematic representations are closely bound up with the individual self."[2] Herbert Read, in his penetrating analysis, went far beyond a distinction between visual and non-visual experiences in child art. He showed in great detail that " the individual schema expresses the psychological constitution of the child."[3] Far beyond a mere typological distinction Herbert Read in his book lays down a basic philosophy which profoundly influenced the thinking of teachers, particularly those in Art Education.

[1] Read, Herbert, *Education Through Art*, Faber and Faber, 1943.
[2] Lowenfeld, Viktor, *The Nature of Creative Activity*, p. 22.
[3] *Op. cit.*, p. 22.

Natalie Cole in her book, *The Arts in the Classroom*,[1] still uses mere intuitive approaches, much as Franz Cizek did many years ago in Vienna. The final product—child art—and not the child stands in the foreground of the discussion. Few other books appeared in the field of art education, more in the direction of General Education. Most outstanding among those is *Art Today*[2] which tries to establish, more on a horizontal line, an understanding of the interrelationships in the arts without penetrating deeply into any area. In 1942 Victor D'Amico published his *Creative Teaching in Art*[3] in which he convincingly and with his great sincerity as an educator advocates methods of approach which place the process of creating above the significance of the final product. Several other books appeared with no or little bearing on our subject. In 1947 *Creative and Mental Growth*[4] appeared. Most of my text is based on the findings laid down in *The Nature of Creative Activity*. It is with a humble feeling that I can make the statement that the basic ideas expressed in both publications have been widely accepted. The concept that the art expression of the child is intimately bound up with his growth is the generally accepted concept in art education today. It has been advocated as the principle aim of creative teaching at the Midcentury White House Conference for Children and Youth in Washington, D.C., U.S.A. It has been included in the official courses of study of many of the States in the Union. Before all it has become a part of the thinking of an overwhelming number of teachers in the English-speaking countries. It is self-evident that such concepts grow out of the thinking and working of many individuals. I am deeply indebted to them all.

While the meaning of art education for the growth of the child and the development of his personality is generally accepted in the schools for the normal sighted, it has not yet penetrated the thick walls of most of our institutions for the

[1] Cole, Natalie, *The Arts in the Classroom*, John D. Day Co., 1940.
[2] Faulkner, Ray, Ziegfeld, Edwin, and Hill, *Art Today*, Henry Holt & Co., 1941.
[3] D'Amico, Victor, *Creative Teaching in Art*, Int'l. Textbook Co., 1942.
[4] Lowenfeld, Viktor, *Creative and Mental Growth*, Macmillan Co., 1947, revised edition. 1951.

blind. Creative art for the blind is still considered as misleading the blind and diverting them from the preparation for the vocations which they will use to earn their living. That they can earn it better as well adjusted individuals—and that creative activity used as a promoter of growth helps them in their adjustments—has not yet been understood by most of those responsible for the education of the handicapped. Every handicap is connected with a greater or lesser detachment from the environment depending on the degree and kind of handicap.[1] This is true for emotional and mental, as well as physical or even social handicaps. Whether we can in the individual case speak of a handicap depends not only on the degree of handicap but even more on the individual and his ability to adjust. Two individuals with the same degree of physical handicap may differ widely in their detachment from their environments. We may consider two types of detachments : the *objective detachment*, which is the degree of handicap ; and the *subjective detachment*, which is the degree by which the individual suffers from his handicap. Blindness, to give an example, can mean a serious handicap for one who continuously longs for sight and thus remains unaware of his own particular qualities. For another it may become a part of his personality, as it were. He not only adjusts to his blindness, but uses all opportunities to enrich his life. His subjective detachment has almost ceased to exist. All who have worked in institutions for the blind know of these differences. Yet, being unable to see is not always an inhibitory factor. On the contrary, as has been proven in this and other publications, it may become the basis of a specific and unique creativeness. In it there is not only a distinct difference from visual art expression, but also a specific approach to creative art. This specific approach results from the need of building up a whole image out of partial impressions. What the blind individual cannot always achieve in life he can do in his creative work : out of the many partial impressions he builds up a " whole ". What a release it must be when he

[1] Lowenfeld, Berthold, *Psychological Aspects of Blindness*, Ency. of Psychology, Philosophical Library, 1946, N.Y.

can identify himself with his own work without interference in his mode of expression. Through his continuous contact and establishment of relationships between his thinking and the realization of it in his work he obviously improves his ability to integrate partial impressions into a " whole ". This ability surely is not confined only to his creative work, but reflects upon the emotional and mental growth of the individual in general. It affects his ability to orient in space, for spatial orientation greatly consists of integrating partial impressions. As it affects his ability for orientation it helps him to overcome his detachments. As he faces himself through his creative activity in his work, he gains self confidence and emotional release.

Attempts have been made to recognize modelling as a " subject " in the curricula of a few institutions for the blind. But there remains the sad and depressing experience that the " seeing taste " of physically normal " educators " determines the way of expression of the blind. It is time to realize that the most primitive creative work born in the mind of a blind individual and produced with his own hands is of greater value for his growth than the most effective imitation.

Psychological Implications : It is quite clear that psycholgical implications cannot be entirely separated from the educational. Herbert Read has shown us in his work how the one is closely interwoven with the other. Yet, when we deal with tests and measurements in regard to personality characteristics, we can make such a distinction. This is precisely the type of work with which I have concerned myself. In the course of the study with which this book deals it has been found that imaginative activity, including the ability to give objective reference to creations of the imagination, by no means depends upon the capacity for perceptive observations. It is quite obvious that it would disturb and greatly inhibit a visually minded person to be stimulated only by means of haptic impressions, or to be asked not to use sight and orient himself only by means of touch, bodily feelings, muscular sensations, and kinæsthetic fusions. It is, however, not so clear that " seeing " may also become an inhibitory factor when forced upon an individual who does not use his visual experiences for creative work.

Further studies have shown that the distinction which is true for creative types can also be made among individuals in general. An extreme haptical type of individual would be a normal sighted person who uses his eyes only when he is compelled to do so ; otherwise he reacts as would a blind person who is entirely dependent upon touch and kinaesthesis. An extreme visually minded person, on the other hand, is one who is entirely lost in the dark, one who depends completely on his visual experiences of the outside world.

It is evident that most persons fall between these two extreme types. In order to establish the ratio of both types I designed " Tests for Visual and Haptical Aptitudes ".[1] From 1128 reactions received, 47 per cent of the subjects were clearly visual, 23 per cent were haptic and 30 per cent either received a score which was below the line where a clear identification was possible or was otherwise not identifiable. In other words, approximately half of the individuals tested reacted visually, whereas not quite a fourth reacted haptically. Thus it would appear that, so far as our evidence goes, one among four individuals depends upon touch and kinaesthesis rather than upon vision.

This seemed to me also of some significance in regard to the proper choice of occupations. There are occupations in which visual control is not only impossible but would interfere with the efficiency of the worker ; mechanical jobs which are done inside a case with the hands as the only control, work in the darkness, work on switch-boards. It is also clear that there are occupations which place the main emphasis on the use of the eyes. They deal with occular observation, estimation of distance, orientation, surveying. Certainly a great number of occupations require both abilities ; yet it is often possible to determine which of these aptitudes is dominant and of greater importance.

It has been demonstrated in this book that one of the peculiarities of the perception of space of the blind and the

---

[1] Lowenfeld, Viktor, *Tests for Visual and Haptical Aptitudes*, The American Journal of Psychology, Vol. 58, No. 1., 1945.

partially blind is that both arrive at their image only through a constructive synthesis out of partial impressions. One factor in visual observation is the ability to first see the whole without the awareness of details, then to analyze it into detailed or partial impressions and to build these parts up again into a new synthesis of the whole. We see first the general shape of a tree, then the single leaves, the twigs, the branches, the trunk, and then finally everything incorporated in the synthesis of the whole tree. Partial impressions thus are integrated into a simultaneous image. Since this process is also of utmost importance for the ability to orient in space I designed a test on the " Integration of Successive Impressions." This test, used by the U.S. Army Air Forces, was to me one of the most fascinating psychological implications of the art of the blind.

There are many more psychological implications. I wanted only to touch upon the ones which seemed to me most important. The psychological implications for the blind have largely been discussed under the educational implications.

Aesthetic Implications : By far the most outstanding work which deals with the aesthetic implications of the art of the blind and partially blind remains the contribution which Ludwig Münz previously made.[1] It has been extensively discussed in this book. Herbert Read[2] has given us the broad philosophy under which our findings have received new perspective. Louis Danz[3] in his *Personal Revolution and Picasso* used many findings of this book—even in their original wordings—to " explain aesthetic principles " in a rather naive form. In his book he gives us an account of how haptic sensations revealed to him the nature of the art of Picasso. In 1950 G. Révész[4] published " for the first time " his *Psychology and Art of the Blind*, previously published under a different name.[5] He writes rather presumptuously,

[1] Münz, Ludwig, and Lowenfeld, Viktor, *Plastische Arbeiten Blinder*, R. M. Rohrer, 1934.
[2] *Op. cit.*
[3] Danz, Louis, *Personal Revolution and Picasso*, Longmans, Green & Co., N.Y., 1941.
[4] Révész, G., *Psychology and Art of the Blind*, Longmans, Green & Co., 1950.
[5] Révész, G., *Die Formenwelt des Tastsinnes*, Martinus Nijhoff, The Hague, 1938.

" I am offering the first treatise on tactile aesthetics, the first foundation for the aesthetics and Art of the Blind ". Throughout his book, however, he uses the illustrations of previously published material.

After a discussion of the fundamental problems of space perception Révész develops a theory strongly leaning toward the one of Lowenfeld and Münz in which he distinguishes between the haptic of the seeing (" optified haptics ") and the haptic of the blind (" pure autonomous haptic "). He points out that the seeing translate their tactile perceptions into visual ones—they optify ; while the blind rely on their tactile perceptions as such. Révész criticizes the fact that "optical questions and methods governed the whole field of haptics and the Psychology of the Blind," but when it comes to an evaluation of haptic aesthetics in the sculptures of the blind he not only accepts the judgment of seeing person, but derives from their opinions the conclusion that they are " unartistic personal expression of subjective experiences, and are not governed by any canons of form." This conclusion is derived from a statement " that the autoplastic (haptic) method of representation is entirely unsuitable for expressing emotions and feelings in a manner *generally* understandable." To write such value judgments at a time when modern art in its strong individual modes of expression has taught us that the degree of communicability by no means is an expression of artistic value is more than surprising, especially, in an analysis on tactile aesthetics.

It is somehow the tragic fate of the author to postulate an " autonomous way of treating the haptic," but to succumb to his own subjective visual experiences. He writes : " We can make the statement that the haptic is entirely independent of the sense of vision and develops its world by means of its own laws." In spite of that we find throughout the book visual aesthetic evaluations applied to haptic form concepts.

At the end of this preface I want to express my deep felt gratitude to the publishers Routledge and Kegan Paul Ltd., who published the first edition at a time when Europe was in turmoil, exactly on the day when Hitler moved into my home city of Vienna, and who again undertake to publish the second edition in a time of crisis.

VIKTOR LOWENFELD.

December, 1951.

FORMER CONCEPTIONS ABOUT THE ART OF THE BLIND

The literature which deals with the creative activities of the blind or the weak sighted is exceptionally meagre. In 1931 Wilhelm Voss (Kiel) wrote *Subjektive und Objecktive Aufbauelemente in den Zeichnungen Blinder*.[1] The same author also published an article, "*bildmässiges Zeichnen blinder Kinder*," which has much the same content.[2] His work contains many important facts and conclusions but I believe that the technical procedure used by him, which consisted in putting together a line point by point, necessarily and from the outset excludes much that seems to me particularly important in the normal drawing of children.[3] Drawings obtained in this way obviously cannot get beyond a certain primitive stage. Like so many before and after him Voss makes the mistake of attributing the dominating role in creative activity to the hand as the organ of touch. Speaking of a subject's "inner pictures," he says : "they reside in his hand ; with his fingers he feels objects, and with them he also thinks." He is here confusing production and reproduction. Certainly the hand is the mediator for concepts arrived at by touch and this means that the conception which a blind child has of an object is a constructive synthesis of the different partial impressions received by touch. But when forms are being *created* matters are quite otherwise.[4] As a result of his work Voss comes to the conclusion that the blind have a tendency towards ' stereotyped ' forms : "The blind man possesses only one rigid symbol for each object. He is lacking in all the preconditions necessary for expressing motion by typical presentations."

---

[1] Published by the *psychologisch aesthetische Forschungsgesellschaft*, Hamburg.

[2] *Kunst u. Jugend*. Deutsche Blätter für Zeichenkunst und Werkunterricht, xi, 1931. Stuttgart : E. Hardt.

[3] Voss allowed the children to use a ruler with which to prick holes with a pin into a piece of paper lying on a cushion filled with sawdust.

[4] Cf. L. Münz, V. Lowenfeld : *Plastische Arbeiten Blinder* (hereafter referred to as Münz-Lowenfeld, P.A.B. Also Lowenfeld, *Die Entstehung der Plastik*.

" With moving hands he touches bodies at rest," or, " The resting hand lies on an object in motion." In other words, Voss completely leaves out of account that creative activity which springs from body sensations and from the fact that sensations are bound to the experience of the self.

In the year 1910 an article by Burde on plasticine modelling by blind children appeared in the *Zeitschr. f. angew. Psychol.* His work too, does not get beyond a certain stage of primitive, piece by piece synthesis by the child. W. Matz experimented in a primary school with modelling and also used blind subjects. Like Burde he judges the work according to general æsthetic principles. He talks of " false proportions " in comparing the work of the blind with nature.[1] In his book *Die Kunst des Kindes*, Stuttgart, 1927, Oskar Wulff discusses these experiments as well as a number of others that were conducted in a Silesian Institute for the Blind, probably with a ' naturalistic ', i.e. false bias. He comes to the conclusion that " the touch sensations of the finger tips are far inferior as regards fineness to those of the muscles of the eye, by the combination of which with visual impressions the visual concept probably first grows.[2] It is the eyes that regulate the progress of work in those of normal sight, whereas the blind who touch one part after another cannot get beyond a mere piecemeal construction ". " The visual impressions, by being repeated and integrated with other sense impressions, give rise to the visual image and because the visual impression is lacking the blind are denied the possibility of testing the agreement of the parts among each other and the structure of a composition as a whole." In these quotations Wulff, too, completely neglects that vital creative process which springs from the body sensations and overlooks the fact that " putting together the separate parts " does not exclude a conception of the work as a whole. Though in another part of his book he admits the importance

---

[1] Matz, W., " Zeichen- und Modellierversuche an Volksschülern, Taubstum men und Blinden," *Zeitschr. f. angew. Psychol.*, 1915.

[2] O. Wulff calls the twodimensional image or concept ' visual form ' since strictly speaking it is the only one which corresponds to a ' picture ', whereas the threedimensional image he calls ' visual concept '.

of body sensations—but only for modelling—he does not see the extreme importance in other connections of this mode of experiencing form. Indeed, he says " The creative will which arises out of the sensations of the body and the memory of touch and muscular sensations is not capable of a finer development as long as the visual image with which they fuse does not develop to full clarity ".

It was not until my classes produced plastic work for the first time that it was possible to give any proof of the creative possibilities of the blind. The reader is referred to the book by Ludwig Münz and Victor Lowenfeld *Plastische Arbeiten Blinder*, Brünn, 1934. In this Münz gives a very full and thorough analysis, on the lines of Gestalt Psychology, of current views about the creative abilities of the blind. He defines and discusses three conceptions of the space and form experience of the blind. First, " the generally rejected view of Herder who maintains that the structure of the form and space experience of the blind is related to that of children and primitive peoples. Secondly, that of Theodor Heller and Steinberg who agree that the form and space experience of the blind in principle coincides to a large extent with that of the normal sighted but who are unable to say anything further about its structure. And thirdly, the conception of the Wittmann-Senden group, which denies that beyond the visual there can be any experience of form and space." The work carried out by the blind in my classes provided a broader basis for Münz's investigations of the understanding of the conceptions of form and space by the blind, and of the creative sources of their modelling. In the course of investigations to be discussed in this book we shall have occasion to refer frequently to this basic work on the psychology of the blind.[1]

[1] As this work was going to press Professor G. Révész sent me a proof of the chapter on " Modelling achievements of the congenitally blind " from his book *Die Formenwelt des Tastsinns*. Unfortunately it came too late for me to discuss in detail. I should, however, like to say that the statement printed in italics, at the beginning of the chapter, that " the creative process obeys essentially the same rules as the process of perception when three-dimensional objects are being touched ", and which the author maintains is a result of my modelling experiments with the blind, does not agree with

I turned particularly to the art of children first because of the relation of the form experience of the blind to that of children and secondly because I have studied the ontogenetic development of drawing by the weak sighted. Particular attention is devoted to that part of this very wide field which best illustrates its connection with the creative modes of the blind and weak sighted. The literature about the art of children is extensive but similar in approach. In it the phenomenon of *autoplastic* creation and the expression of valuing tendencies in drawing, i.e. the phenomenon of ' ego-linkage ', has been almost wholly neglected. I have therefore devoted particular attention to the investigation of the separation of the visual from the tactile and kinæsthetic spheres of experience.

My investigations approached the phenomenon from two sides. On the one hand I attempted to approach the world of experience and the creative methods of the child from the *individual drawing*. This represents the static and Gestalt psychological discussion of the data. On the other hand I attempted to solve the problem dynamically by investigating the way in which development takes place. The development of drawing in the individual child and the general stages of development characteristic of different ages will be investigated separately. In this connection I studied as a developmental series the treatment of one theme from the fifth to the fifteenth year. From each age group I obtained about 40 drawings which permitted me to draw some conclusions about the psychology of form. The choice of a theme was dictated by the fact that I wished to obtain material for the development of visual as well as of tactile and kinæsthetic experiences of form and feeling.

When we regard our material in this way, many things hitherto dismissed in the art of children as " childish mistakes " take on meaning. William Stern [1] says, " originally the child sees not only with his eyes but with

my observations and scientific conclusions. His way of putting it is irreconcilable with an autoplastic expressive experience o ·form. Révész, however, continues as follows : " This unexpected agreement gives special force to our discussions about the haptic perception of form."

[1] *Psychologie der frühen Kindheit*, Leipzig, 1930.

his whole person." Unfortunately he fails to give a convincing proof for the validity of this hypothesis. But that he is not concerned with autoplastic creations, may be seen from the following quotation : " The eye merely forms the gateway for a total experience which is strongly tinged with expression." In his later discussions Stern lays particular emphasis upon the conceptual aspect. " For the child draws what it means, thinks and knows, not what it sees." He thus recognizes that over emphases which show themselves in the exaggeration of proportions, have expressive importance but he does not go so far as to give a thorough phenomeno-logical discussion. Karl Bühler [1] says, " the sustaining principle of *all kinds* of pictorial representation is the relation of similarity between that which has been depicted in the drawing, and the object which it represents. The simplest and in many respects paradigmatic type of representation is ' the picture ' in the narrower sense of the word. It corresponds to its object because of the relationships of colour and shape that obtain between them."

But surely this formulation is true only of visual art. It does not hold for those representations of expression which spring from the autoplastic experience of form. Since the art of children consists of so many non-visual components this conclusion of Bühler shows that he regards the eye as the dominating factor in experience. His view that " the little artist is far more of a symbolist than a naturalist " does not contradict this.[2] In another place Bühler says that " the person who is unskilled in drawing shows in arriving at his perception and images of form a preference for certain basic ways of looking at objects". These aspects he calls *orthoscopic views.*[3] I mention these conceptions of

[1] *Die Geistige Entwickiung des Kindes,* Jena, 6th edn., 1930.
[2] The chapter on " The analysis of the act of drawing " confirms this view in that Bühler speaks of ' disproportions of size ' without explaining these. Most of Bühler's views are to be found in a condensed form in Ch. V, *The Mental Development of the Child,* Kegan Paul, 1930.
[3] In *Die Entwicklung des plastischen Gestaltens vorschulpflichtiger Kinder* Otto Krauter maintains that we cannot properly speak of ' views ' in connection with orthoscopic pictures : " when we speak of different ' views ' that is merely a device found useful in the vocabulary of the adult." Nevertheless he does point out that it would be a mistake to assume that the orthoscopic views are preferred because they are more often experienced. He says :

Bühler because even weak sighted, almost blind children who are never able to get a clear visual impression of a large object (cf. Table II) draw 'orthoscopic views'. Consequently, the drawing of orthoscopic pictures cannot have anything to do with visual experience, i.e. with 'preferred basic views'. We shall content ourselves here with this general assertion. In the course of the investigation we shall have occasion to go further into this matter and also to refer frequently to the extremely important problems developed in the work of Bühler.

"All artistic ability has its root in universal human dispositions. It is determined only by the exceptional intensification of the abilities of certain individual senses. Consequently we must first inquire what the motive forces are." This sentence comes at the beginning of the chapter on "the psychic roots of the formation of visual images and of drawings ", in the book, *Die Kunst des Kindes*, by O. Wulff. Throughout this book, in which the development of children's drawings is dealt with from the earliest beginnings up to the point where representational art begins, visual *form* and visual *concept* are alternately regarded as the most important. Visual *form* has found its purest artistic expression in silhouette—"In it alone pure visual form has found an independent method of expressing those artistic fantasies whose germ lies in the plane picture and which has freed itself from entanglement with the concept." The visual *concept* (spatial thinking) finds its expression more in plastic art. According to Wulff a representation that is true to appearances must be thought of as being the product of the synthesis of visual form and visual concept.[1] But when we look at plastic work by people who have been blind since birth, what can we say about 'visual form' and

---

"the child *sees* things in continually different aspects. The orthoscopic view is only one among many others." I believe that this also throws light on Bühler's opinion about this problem of form. Cf. *Die geistige Entwicklung des Kindes*, 272 : "I propose the expression ' orthoscopic forms ' with reference to the tendency towards orthogonal localization, i.e. the tendency " to localize visual impressions vertically to the line of sight except where it is counteracted by tendencies towards localization in some other plane " (Jaensch)."

[1] "I call a photograph ' realistic ', and with it every picture which is constructed *according to the principles of photography*, that is, above all with due regard to the perspective of form and size." Bühler, *op. cit.*, p. 119.

' visual concept' ? They, too, frequently come very near to achieving a representation true to appearances. Or, again, what are we to say in this connection about the realistic drawings of the extremely weak sighted Sch. G. (cf. Table I, page 15) ? The existence of such artistic products of the blind or nearly blind must to some extent invalidate Wulff's theory because to be consistent he has to deny that differentiated creative activity is possible for the blind since they lack what he calls the visual form.

Of particular importance for my own work was that of W. Krötzsch.[1] He describes the scribbling stage as one in which differentiated bodily movements are already expressed, and this led me to perceive the close integration with the self of even early infantile modes of expression.

In the vast literature concerned with the laws of children's drawings are many works to which one should refer, such as the pioneer investigations of C. Ricci,[2] the great work of G. Kerschensteiner,[3] the work of Levinstein, Helga Eng, Matz, and G. F. Hartlaub. Where the text demands it I shall refer to them, here I merely want to indicate separately those problems which have arisen out of the most recent investigations.

Through an analysis of the work of the weak sighted which forms the major part of this volume, and from a comparison of this work with that of those who enjoy full vision, my attention was drawn to two types of artists. The investigation showed that these two types exist quite independently of the physiological facts of sight. This fact, together with the presence of similar form symbols in earlier primitive works of art, as well as the similarity of the spatial representation of one of these artistic types with that to be found in the artistic documents of widely different epochs, next led me to turn my attention to Babylonian, Assyrian and Egyptian art. It seemed to me that this particular conception of space found its strongest artistic expression in that art. The connection between the work of the weak-sighted and

---

[1] *Rhythmus und Form in der freien Kinderzeichnung*, Leipzig, 1917.
[2] *L'arte dei Bambini*, Bologna, 1887.
[3] *Die Entwicklung der zeichnerischen Begabung*, 1905.

that of blind people, which is analysed in a separate chapter in this book, also enabled me to draw parallels with primitive art and with the expressive art which L. Münz had already studied in the plastic work of the blind. In the present book we are in addition able to study the ways in which space is represented in drawings and paintings. Consequently further conclusions can be drawn about the common creative types of visual expression.

It is obvious that there is a close relationship between the drawings of children and those of primitive and even archaic art and this theme has frequently enough been treated. Nevertheless the particular standpoint of this book requires a particular and detailed exposition. Gustav Britsch [1] has shown in great detail and in his own way that the conditions of thinking at early stages are frequently the same. He compares the drawings of children of different types with archaic Egyptian and primitive art. But though his philosophic method of analysis is consistent he takes into account only *visual* experiences. Even in the case of representations that are contrary to nature he says "These are not ways of looking at 'nature', i.e. not a set of generally accepted presuppositions, but they are judgements, or possibilities of thinking *about* nature, in other words theories under which the experiences of the true visual sense are subsumed and are thought of as a unity ". Indeed Britsch goes further, and, speaking of the difference between works of art and other scientific conceptions says, " in so far as these conceptions are not directed to the apprehension and intellectual assimilation of the experiences of the sense of sight they are conceptions about things lying outside the artistic nature of the work."

Bühler, too, discusses the relation of the drawings of children to those of primitive peoples. He is particularly concerned with the naturalistic drawings of the most primitive peoples because these display neither the schema of children's drawings as one might have expected nor pass through this stage. He refers to the teachings of Verworn

[1] Gustav Britsch, *Theorie der Bildenden Kunst*, ed. Kornmann. Munich, 1926.

who was the first to recognize that there was a psychological problem here. Bühler raises the question whether we may not in our earliest youth have possessed the faculties, of naturalistic perception. " It is possible " he says, " that this is so. Perhaps the memory of the child is approximately the same as that of the most primitive peoples, up to the time when it begins to speak and to learn to use the first words as names of species." I shall refer in more detail to the theories of both Verworn and Bühler since I believe them to have received confirmation by my own investigations.

The relation of the art of children to that of primitive peoples, the relation of both these to the mode of expression used by the weak sighted and the blind, the common mode of representing space in early and archaic works of art and the presence of the same form symbols and means of expression in the case of emotionally expressive representation, all showed clearly that in these forms of creative activity the experiences of the visual sense had to relinquish their primacy.

It would lead too far were we to subject the art of psychotics to the same phenomenological investigation.[1] Wulff has considered this in connection with the art of children and here we should merely like to point out that in the drawings of psychotics one finds a far higher degree of subjective reference together with many tactile (haptic) form symbols. This may be owing to the fact that psychotics are very much more isolated intellectually from their environment, for in some form or another most mental illnesses consist in the inability to achieve correct relations with the environment.

Whenever an attempt is made to throw light on artistic problems from *one* angle alone, the danger of misunderstanding is great. Nevertheless in this book still another attempt will be made to approach from one aspect a little more closely to the enormous complexity of artistic experience.

[1] Cf. Prinzhorn, *Die Kunst der Geisteskranken.*

Chapter I

THE CONDITIONS FOR THE ABILITY TO DRAW

(a) PHYSICAL BASIS

One might be tempted to believe that the mere physiological ability to see is the only prerequisite for representing plane and spatial objects by means of drawings. This is not so, however, as our investigations will presently show. ' Vision ' is physiologically limited solely by total inability to find one's way about on the paper. To determine the precise degree of visual acuity which allows this orientation is difficult, because it seems to differ from individual to individual and to depend on numerous subsidiary factors. It is clear, however, that the possibility of orientating oneself on the paper as well as of projectively creating a drawing is not necessarily connected directly with the physical degree of visual acuity. Some pupils who have only the barest minimum of visual acuity nevertheless possess an excellent power of expressing themselves through drawing. Some who possess a higher degree of visual capacity cannot use it for projective creative work. There are others about whose visual capacities we are uncertain. Before they can use their physical capacities in the appropriate manner they first have to be trained to see the external world as well as to orientate themselves in it. For still others all training is ineffective although they have the necessary physiological ability. For the purely functional possibilities of drawing, therefore, only two points are important. Inability to draw in spite of physical capacity must be left to a later investigation which will concern itself with the type of artist as well as with his physical habitus. Here I shall confine myself to stating the prerequisites for normal cases, i.e. those in which the physical basis can be freely exploited to unfold the possibilities of drawing. These are

(1) The nature and degree of visual acuity must be such that it allows accurate fixation of a point.

(2) The training of the eye and the nature of its vision must be such that it is possible to follow the direction and goal of a line.

The pupil's ability to orientate himself in the plane of drawing and therefore all possibility of creative development, of whose prerequisites we shall speak next, depends essentially upon these two factors.

(b) PREREQUISITES FOR THE DEVELOPMENT OF CREATIVE CAPACITY

The mere physical ability to orientate oneself on the paper is naturally not enough. The development of the creative power of expression depends largely upon mental factors. Consequently, defects in the mental sphere will also have to be sought. At this point I do not wish to take up fundamental questions about the origin of visual and non-visual concepts and their projection in the form of drawings. This discussion is left to later chapters, but we should note that the ability to project also determines the possibilities of creative development. To provide a basis for such a development it is necessary to remove all inhibitions standing in the way of free creativeness. It is essential therefore to consider some basic pedagogic questions, the answer to which will clearly and concretely reveal the problems that determined the direction taken by the scientific analysis of the task we set ourselves.

Before one can remove inhibitions it is necessary to recognize them as such. Superfluous as this statement may sound it is necessary, in spite of its self-evidence, to place it at the beginning of our discussion. To anticipate somewhat, it should be observed, for example, that it would be completely wrong to attempt to set free the creative powers of a non-visual type of child by trying to remove its 'visual inhibition' and anxiously attempting to familiarise it with visual impressions. One would in fact achieve the exact opposite, just as one would inhibit creative ability by forcing a visualiser to pay special attention to tactile impressions. *Not being able to see, or rather, not noticing visual impressions, is not always an inhibitory factor.* On the contrary, as I hope to show, the very fact of not paying attention to visual impressions becomes the basis of the specific creativeness of a certain type. Therefore, before the way is cleared for the development of creative ability it is essential to ascertain which creative type is involved. The illustrations show that it is supremely important not to use naturalistic modes of expression as the criterion of value, but to free oneself from such conceptions. They show also that the use of such a criterion actually acts as an inhibitor of free creative expression. I hope that nowadays it is no longer necessary to emphasise the most general educational principle, that the teacher should on no account force his particular forms of expression on the child or, worse still, ' improve ' the work of the child by introducing into it some of his own.

In the course of our discussions it will from time to time be unavoidable, wherever the particular circumstances of the theme necessitate it, to point to fundamental educational principles.

Once more, therefore, I would emphasise that the prerequisites for free creativeness are given only when the creative principle has been recognized and carefully tested, and when it is used as the basis for the free development of the will to expression.

Chapter II

DEFINITION OF WEAK SIGHT

(a) PHYSICAL WEAK SIGHT

We speak of physical weak sight when owing to a functional defect of the eye which cannot be corrected, there is a disturbance of the ability to see.

Table I gives information about cases dealt with in this book. In these cases the physical consequences of the functional defect consist in the rapid deterioration of visual acuity at very small distances, in a restriction of the field of vision going far beyond the normal and frequently in the impossibility of visually perceiving tridimensional objects as such. With the causes of these defects of the eye we are not here concerned. They may be left to medical research.

(b) PSYCHOLOGICAL WEAK SIGHT

We understand by psychological weak sight a disturbance of the ability to perceive the environment which cannot be immediately reduced to a physiological defect of the eye. An extreme case of psychological weak sight therefore would be a person having full vision who can neither orientate himself in his environment nor find his way about in it. His eye would be a mere *camera obscura*. The images on the retina would not penetrate consciousness at all or only for brief moments. In this category we must also place those cases of normal sight who are able to use their eyes for perceiving their environment but have no desire to do so. They prefer to get to know their environment by means other than visual. In most cases, however, a certain degree of physiological disability will go hand in hand with psychological disabilities and *vice versa*. We may speak of temporary psychological weak sight where it is possible to improve perception by training. This occurs most often when there is a sudden change in the capacity to see which is not immediately followed by a change in psychological attitude. It is well known, for instance, that those who have recovered their sight through an operation sometimes have for a long time to learn to see before they achieve the capacity of perceiving visual objects.

The restriction of the field of view also leads in many cases to psychological defect. The appended tables show that there are weak sighted persons whose field of view is so restricted that only a small cone of light reaches the retina. Consequently the eye, or rather the head, is in constant movement whenever anything is looked at. The impression of the whole must therefore be made up of numerous partial impressions which are not perceived simultaneously. There are instances in which these partial impressions never fuse into an impression of the whole, partly because of a lack of orientating ability and partly because the partial impressions are blurred and forgotten.

Finally there are weak sighted subjects whose visual capacity is often quite large, but who do not seem to wish to use it. These are the object of the investigations reported in this book. They lack any directed attitude to the visual world. Things which they quite often perceive with ease through the sense of touch are not perceived visually or only with the greatest difficulty, although the physical possibility of perceiving them exists.

I mention here only those cases of psychological weak sight known to me personally, and then only because they are necessary for the understanding of the following chapters. Their enumeration is therefore short and unsystematic and no claim is made that it is exhaustive. An exhaustive treatment would go far beyond the limits of this book and must be left to other sciences.

TABLE I

Name	Date of Birth	Type and Degree of Weak Sight	Distance of Eyes from Work, in cms.	Approximate Diameter of Visual Field When Working, in cms.	Notes
(1) H. A.	1st June, 1920	Congenital amblyopia with atrophy of the optic nerve (not total)	10	12	At first colour blind with respect to complementary colours only. This later almost entirely disappeared.
(2) M. B.	11th Sept., 1918	Congenital cataract of both eyes	5–8	10–12	
(3) Sch. G.	13th April, 1922	Congenital cataract of both eyes. Right eye operated	1½–2	6	
(4) S. Gr.	9th Nov., 1920	Congenital cataract of both eyes	3–6	11	
(5) G. K.	14th Mar., 1920	Congenital cataract of both eyes (history of cataract in the family)	10	12	
(6) J. M.	15th Jan., 1915	Sclerotic Scars both sides with incipient *phthysis bulbi* (after measles in 2nd year)	—	—	Does not use his eyes at all when working
(7) G. St.	31st May, 1919	Neuritic atrophy of the optic nerve	5–7	13	

TABLE II

Name	Date of Birth	Type and Degree of Weak Sight	Distance of Eyes from Work, in cms.	Approximate Diameter of Visual Field When Working, in cms.
(1) A. B.	24th Jan., 1923	Congenital grey cataract of both eyes (operated)	3–5	7
(2) L. B.	25th April, 1925	Congenital grey cataract of both eyes	2–3	5½
(3) D. H.	25th Mar., 1925	Microphthalmus with grey cataract of both eyes (congenital)	2–3	4
(4) G. R.	20th Dec., 1926	Congenital blindness with minimal visibility. Sclerotic Scars following Blennorrhœa at birth	2	3
(5) K. W.	31st Mar., 1928	Congenital Microphthalmus	2	4
(6) A. H.	17th Sept., 1927	Hereditary cataract incident at 4th year	6	6–8
(7) Ch. R.	7th Aug., 1926	Congenital grey cataract of both eyes	1–2	2
(8) R. F.	25th June, 1928	Congenitally weak sight and inflammation of the optic nerve	1	2

CHAPTER III

CHILDREN'S DRAWINGS AS A MEANS OF EXPRESSION, WITH SPECIAL REFERENCE TO HAPTIC AND KINÆSTHETIC PROBLEMS OF FORM

(a) THE SIGNIFICANCE OF THE SCRIBBLING STAGE FOR LATER ARTISTIC DEVELOPMENT

Lack of adequate material prevents me from making a careful investigation of the scribbling stage in weak sighted children. The material presented here begins at the stage which Krötzsch regards as the end of the scribbling stage, i.e., where " the domination of the object " begins. But since all my investigations lead me to believe that the scribbling of the weak sighted can be no different from that of the normal sighted I shall cite and amplify those portions of Krötzsch's work which seem to me important for my own investigation. Krötzsch maintains that the scribbling of children begins as rhythmical movements which are in a sense undifferentiated and uncontrolled. Gradually the child begins to appreciate that there is a relation between the conscious experience of muscular movement and the strokes on the paper. " At first the child moves now the right and then the left hand without criticism or rather without conscious choice using now the correct and now the incorrect end of the pencil. At some point it suddenly perceives the relation between its movement and the permanent mark on the paper. After that it continues to go through the process more and more consciously until, having over and over again observed the relation, it discovers the causal interdependence of movement and effect." It is now, according to Krötzsch, that scribbling proper begins. Up to this point there should be no difference between the scribbling of the normal sighted and the weak sighted, for visual experience only begins to play its part from the time when the relation between rhythmical movement and line is perceived. From now on the separate stages of scribbling will differ in the two cases, for the technical process of drawing is essentially different in the case of the weak sighted child. Krötzsch notes that to begin with the movements affect the whole arm. That is they are controlled to a greater extent by the shoulder than by the elbow. But the scribbling of the weak sighted, about which so far as I know there have been no investigations, must proceed somewhat differently. The drawings illustrated here are already determined by objects but are nevertheless still closely related to the scribbling stage. The act of drawing proceeds as follows. The eye is very close to the paper, 1-2 cms. (cf. Table II). Since the movements of the hand or the arm have all the time to be under the control of the eye, it is not only the arm or the hand which is in motion but, according to my observations, the whole upper part of the body, not only the head. Although the size of the visual field would enable the child to go through these movements in stages, it nevertheless follows the line through with its whole body. This slows down the rhythmical movement considerably so that one could hardly speak of a " swinging scribble " such as Helga Eng has observed and noted as a developmental stage.[1] Future investigations will have to decide whether the movement in the case of the weak sighted is as Krötzsch describes it, " at first with broad and simple impulses, then becoming more differentiated with shorter and multiple impulses," and whether " forms are at first made in almost straight lines and without interruptions, subject only to external force ; then broken and more and more controlled in force ; then by circular lines and, finally, in spirals." However, Krötzsch's assertion that the scribbles are a true reproduction of the movement, will certainly be true here also. We shall not, however, find agreement about the age at which the various stages appear. As regards the shapes themselves, however, these facts are unimportant since the dates which Krötzsch gives vary within wide individual limits even for the normal sighted. Here we need

[1] Eng, Helga, " Kinderzeichnen," *Zeitschr. f. angew. Psychol.*, Beiheft 29. *The Psychology of Children's Drawings*, London, Kegan Paul, 1931.

merely note that in the later development of their ability to draw the weak sighted fall behind the full sighted.

I do not agree fully with Krötzsch in his assertion that the giving of names to the scribbles—which is at first done *after* the scribble has been completed—is the result of adult influence. On the contrary, as has been shown by my recent experimentations, the " Naming of Scribbling " represents one of the most important stages in human development. *It indicates a change of thinking from a mere kinaesthetic to an imaginative.* Since most of our concrete thinking refers in one way or another to imagery—the thinking in terms of mental pictures—I consider this stage in the child's development a most important one. While the child previously was concerned with motions only, he now refers in his scribbling to mental pictures.[1]

We now arrive at the stage the development of which I am able to illustrate by means of concrete examples. For data about the Subjects the reader is referred to Tables I and II. Fig. 1 shows G's first drawing of " a man ". It is important to note that when she made this drawing she, like the other children, was of an age at which this stage has normally been long transcended. But as this was the first time G. took to drawing, she went through the stages of development corresponding to earlier ages and then proceeded by a series of jumps to attain the stage appropriate to her age.

To begin with she executed circular motions with her arm, moving her trunk at the same time and in the same rhythm. The irregular circular scribbles which she thus produced she named " the head ". The scribbling was repeated below the head in larger rhythms and named " body ". To left and right two open lines indicated the arms whilst the feet were drawn as continuations of the circular or spiral scribbling constituting the body. A closed line was designated " house " and the circles within it as windows and doors. The two horizontal strokes she called " steps ". Afterwards, whilst explaining her drawing, she said, " he

---

[1] See Lowenfeld, Viktor, *Creative and Mental Growth*, The Macmillan Co., New York, 1951. (Revised Edition).

is just going into the house." This clearly shows that she had not only appreciated a causal connection but also wished to tell a story. This is evidence that ' telling a story by means of drawing ' does not occur until a later age, as L. Potpeschnigg maintains.

Fig. 2 shows the second stage through which her drawing passed. She not only drew the divisions between the head and the trunk more clearly but made *circular* motions while drawing the head and *longitudinal* scribbles while drawing the body, to characterize, as it were, the different *extensions* of head and body. For some time she was satisfied with this representation of a man, as it seemed to her to contain all essentials. After continual repetition the schema suddenly developed out of this scribbling and she remained at the level of the schema for a long time.

It is extraordinarily interesting how in a flash she begins to abstract a line from the previous scribbling. The circular scribbles become a schematic line for the head which expresses her experience of the form of the head, while out of the longitudinal scribblings of the body the line develops which for her symbolises the extension of the body. This is how we must understand the meaning both of scribbling and of the schema. The former looses more and more the rhythmical relation between bodily movements and formal pattern to make way for the relation to the object. A different mode of drawing begins : the *conscious* creation of form.

Fig. 3 shows the other group the type of whose experience I have been able to follow. The representations take the same form, but the underlying experience is different. Again, out of the apparently meaningless scribbles the abstraction of the object proceeds further and further. But in this case it is not the circumference, the head, which is drawn first and has the parts added to it subsequently, but the parts are drawn first and out of them the whole is put together. I am reluctant to dismiss this by calling one way of drawing ' analytic ' and the other ' synthetic '. I am not concerned with verbal matters but with the mode of experiencing form, which goes far deeper. Perhaps it would be better to say that we are concerned with the question Was the

world there first and were all things created for it ? or Were
the elements of life there first and the world for them merely
the necessary playground ? Would it not be true to say
that the one is concerned with drawing the eyes, the nose
and the mouth as elements in the head, whereas for the other
these elements have become foci of experiences ? The eyes
are there to see, the nose to smell, the mouth for speech,
food and so on. They come first and are important in his life.
Only after they had received the ' correct ' order did they
receive their habitation—the line enclosing the head (fig. 4).
Within this frame of reference the representation gradually
receives a schematic formulation, which, repeated with many
variations and after numerous aberrations, comes to a stand-
still. This *pre-schematic stage* of children's drawings is
characterized by a constant search for a method of representing form. As yet it has not received a fixed aspect and we
see at this stage, in particular, the greatest variety of form
symbols representing one and the same object. Gradually
the child creates its own expressive symbols for every form.
Once again the mode of drawing has reached a turning point.
Schematic drawing begins to predominate and to become the
means of expression and communication for the whole of
the child's experience of form.

(b) THE CONCEPT OF THE SCHEMA IN THE DRAWINGS OF CHILDREN

The child sees the world differently from the way in which
it draws it. It is from this discrepancy between a representation and the thing represented that research has to draw its
inferences. The child's world of experience is so many sided
that we cannot rest content with the mere statement that
the child draws in symbols, in other words introduces
certain signs for objects perceived through the senses
(irrespective of whether these have been obtained visually,
by touch, or acoustically) and by continual repetition gives
to these signs a generalized significance, valid within its own
sphere.[1] We need to investigate these signs which, by

[1] " The Child is far more of a symbolist than a realist," K. Bühler, *Mental Development of the Child.*

repetition, become blunted for individual experience and crystallise into the schema. I shall use the term schema only when within the language of form created by the child we are unable to perceive further changes.[1] As W. Stern has pointed out, it is not in the least necessary that the lines of the schema should have any similarity with the contents represented.   For instance, a tactile experience whose representation in the form of a symbol has nothing whatever to do with external ' similarity ' can just as easily find a place in the schema as a rhythmical movement, which is frequently represented by a wavy line. It is therefore always necessary to question ourselves about the origin of the lines in a schema.   When we remember that as we have seen in the previous chapter, the development of the schematic line frequently has its origin in scribbling, we can understand that in the schema are already reflected some of the personal characteristics of the child.

Thus I noticed that the schema of the human figure developed by a crippled child of normal sight was distorted on the side corresponding to its own defect.

But the individuality of the schema has its roots not only in the body, in autoplastic experience. In many cases it expresses the psychological constitution of the child.   In the schema of an anxious child of delicate sensibilities I could trace this anxiety in the round, unclosed, uncertain lines just as much as I could find the characteristic resoluteness of another child in its rectangular representation of the body. Both schemas seem to me characteristic of the child's total personality structure.   These facts show clearly that *even the earliest schematic representations are closely bound up with the individual self.* They are not arbitrary signs but are intimately related to both the bodily and the mental constitution.   It would be extremely interesting to make a deeper study of these interrelations.

What we have said about the human schema is very largely true of the schematic representation of objects as well

---

[1] W. Stern defines the *schema* as follows : " A schema is a form in which a content of thought is represented by means of natural symbols." *Psychology of Early Youth.*

as of space.   We can speak of schemata whenever the representation of an object has become stereotyped and is repeated in the same form.   The schema, too, can originate in non-visual experience.   In fact we are compelled to assume that for the most part they have a non-visual origin, because we see the same formations in the drawings of weak sighted and of normal sighted children.   However, this is not the place for discussing the psychology of the development of different forms because for the moment we are concerned only with the concept of the schema.   We speak of a space schema when space is represented by some signs or other which, through repetition, assume a constant meaning in the drawings of a child.   That lines have a purely symbolic value becomes plainer still when we consider the representation of space.   Here, because the child lacks facilities for threedimensional representation, it is frequently forced to introduce lines that are nothing but individual symbols. Consequently the space schema is almost entirely abstract and has only an indirect connection with reality.

(*c*) THE SCHEMA AS A MODIFIABLE EXPRESSIVE SYMBOL IN
THE DRAWINGS OF CHILDREN

(1) *The Human Schema*

I use the term *pure* schematic representation in cases where there appears to be no further representational intention beyond that which is represented.   Where such a further intention is present one can no longer speak of a pure schema. Conversely, a study of the kind of modification undergone by the schema, allows us to understand the *intention* underlying the representation.   It seems to me that this method is of importance not only to the psychologist but to the teacher who ought, by this means, to study the effects of his teaching on the development of the capacity for drawing. We shall find a pure schema in a child's drawing whenever the child in its representation confines itself to the object : " That is a tree ; that is a man."   When he says, " this man is big and this one is small," the modifiability of the schema, i.e. the way in which the child expresses ' larger ' or 'smaller', allows us to draw certain conclusions. I got the children to draw a large and a small man. The large man was represented by a simple enlargement of the schema. Then I got them to draw a small man and said that he was now getting older and was growing until he became as large as the man who previously had been drawn as ' large '. The child was then asked to draw the ' grown ' man. I observed that some children drew the body larger in successive stages while they left the feet the same size. In other words ' growing larger ' was kinetically represented by the schema.

The deviations from the rigid schema can be followed in two directions. They can express a *value emphasis*, or, in the case of the human schema, they can spring from body experiences. That is, their nature can be *expressive* or can be derived from the experience of the body or of muscular sensations.[1] When my son was five years old he usually represented the mouth by means of a horizontal line. But when he drew a ' cannibal '—which to him meant nothing more than a wild man—he drew an elongated rectangle with pointed ' teeth ' (fig. 5). In other words, because it was emphasized the mouth received a different symbol. We can perceive the modification of the schema even more clearly in the drawings of the nearly blind A. B. (No. 1, Table II). In his inflexible schema (i.e. unemphasised) he drew the mouth merely as a horizontal line and frequently left it out altogether (figs. 6 *a* and *b*). When he wished to depict someone who was calling out, the mouth received an independent symbol by being drawn at the lower edge of the face. It had, as it were, been ' folded ' outwards. It is as though the mouth which is pushed forward when shouting had in this way received its formal representation.

We come now to the second type of experiences that find their expression in drawing. A. H. (Table II, 6) drew a man, who in spite of the greatest exertion was unable to lift a heavy load, with exaggeratedly long arms. He had the feeling that the great effort, which nevertheless was not enough to lift the load, was pulling out his arms. When the

[1] By "deviations from the schema" I mean only deviations from the schema drawn by an individual child.

man had at last succeeded in lifting the load and in carrying it, A. H. drew the arms small but thick and shaded them. We see here how the bodily experience which had absorbed his attention while he was drawing manifested itself. Stretching of the arms was expressed by the overstressed length, while the tension of the muscles found its symbolic expression in the thickening and shading of the lines representing the arms (fig. 7). I made my pupils draw children who were trying to catch each other and found that in all cases the arm which was stretched out was strongly exaggerated whereas the other arm appeared normal or even diminished (fig. 8). K. indeed detached the ' catching arm ' completely from the body, as though he wished to hurl it after the other person, while the arms of the person who was being caught were left out altogether (fig. 9). The significance of this phenomenon will be discussed later. At this point I content myself merely with drawing attention to the facts.

Out of the great wealth of material at my disposal, I have chosen these few convincing illustrations to show characteristic cases of expressive modifications of the schema. *The schema is thus never a rigid symbol.* Indeed, we have seen that *we can understand the immediate force of the experiences from the very way in which the schema is modified.*

We are not here concerned with the stages undergone by the schema in the course of individual development. Those changes have a totally different origin and will be discussed in a different place.

(2) *The Space Schema*

In the earliest drawings of children the interrelations of things in space are not subject to any laws. They are to a high degree conditioned by value judgments. It is only when the ' base line ' is introduced that we are entitled to speak of a space schema. It shows the child's first intention for order in space. This line represents at once basis, plane and space. That is, it is merely a sign or symbol for expressing them. Although the mode of representing objects in space, which begins as a mixture of plan and front elevation, clearly expresses the intention to create a spatial composition, we cannot yet speak of a generally valid set of laws. The schema here is an entirely individual one. Here too, we shall use the term pure schema only in cases where frequent repetition has crystallised the original experience into a constant formal representation. From now on this ' crystallized formal representation ' becomes the symbol for the corresponding spatial conception. I can remember how intense K's experience was when he for the first time drew a street by ' folding over ' the houses on both sides.[1] From then onwards this became his usual method of representing a street. It became more and more mechanical. Robbed of its original experience it came to be nothing more than a symbol for ' street '. But whenever his drawing was governed by some special intention—if he was drawing a particular street or place, or when the street became the scene of a particular action—he deviated from his usual rigid schema and the whole street achieved a new expression. Indeed, I frequently observed that through such changes the crystallised schema awoke to new life.

I mention this observation particularly because it seems to have a fruitful educational application. The longer the teacher is able to prevent this petrifaction, the more opportunities he can create for strengthening the child's control over new forms, the richer its later powers of expression will be. Here, again, we see that the modifications of the schema are brought about by new intentions. These ' intentions to represent things ' will be discussed in greater detail in the following chapters.

(d) THE DEVELOPMENT OF THE REPRESENTATION OF MAN
(1) *Inflexible Schematic Representation*

By an inflexible schematic representation of man I mean that representation which is obtained when one abstracts the intention to represent from that which is represented.

[1] ' Folding over ' should not be taken in its geometrical sense. The term is used to describe that particular type of drawing by means of which the child wishes to express its conception of spatial relations. In this sense, therefore, one cannot really speak of ' folding over '. I shall keep the term, however, for lack of a better one.

This 'inflexible schema' therefore is a more or less un-conscious abstraction of that which it is intended to represent. The schema goes through a number of phases which differ from individual to individual according to his age, his mental state, and his knowledge. As it does not seem to me of importance for this book to investigate this development, which has already been discussed by numerous other writers, I shall merely point out the characteristic peculiarities of the different schemata.

Broadly, we may note as characteristic in the representa-tion of the face that it develops from the frontal drawing, with dots for eyes, a vertical line for nose, a horizontal one for mouth, via a mixed form containing the nose at the side, to the profile proper. In the course of this development the individual representative symbols become more and more differentiated. In course of time the eye frequently becomes a dot with a semicircular line over it indicating the eyebrow, and later still the eye-ball is represented as a circle and the pupil as a point within the circle. Out of this the eye as an ellipse is frequently developed and this is then surrounded with radial eye lashes. The pupil in the centre becomes more pronounced and is drawn as a small circle. The representative symbol for nose also goes through many stages in the course of development. It should be emphasised once more, however, that these developmental stages in no way follow fixed laws. Not every child necessarily draws the mixed form with the nose at the side, any more than it necessarily goes through the various stages of representing the eye. These are simply characteristic forms which may occur in the course of development. It would be of course extremely interesting to study the circumstances under which the different kinds of representative symbols arise. For example, as a representation for the nose, I have found in addition to the vertical stroke, merely two points for the nostrils, a rectangle with two small vertical strokes in the lower portion of the drawing, or an angle to the left or to the right. The lower part of the nose with the nostrils is occasionally represented by a triangle folded over towards the top and in the lateral mixed form the nose is sometimes drawn as an independent part and sometimes developed out of the profile. In the case of the mouth I have observed the following characteristic expressive symbols : a horizontal line, two parallel lines sometimes connected by means of vertical strokes (teeth), a single line with a small vertical line on it, a rectangle containing small triangles to indicate the teeth, an oval or circle with radial strokes for teeth.

In the case of the whole figure my observations again show that no generally valid rule can be enunciated. In almost all cases the starting point is a relatively ordered conception of " head to feet ", though even this is not an invariable rule. Every child goes through its own individual development. For example, when my son was four and a half years old, and for the first time drew ' correctly ' co-ordinated pictures, I could clearly perceive his desire to represent conceptual relations. Fig. 62 shows that he drew separate circles for chest, stomach, and body. Later, at the age of five, he drew a simple representative symbol for the trunk and depicted it as an ellipse. In addition I found the following forms representing ' body '. A vertical line, two lines which were continued to represent the feet, a rectangle, an oval, a trapezium with the base at the top or bottom and even a triangle.

In the inflexible schema, the most frequent representation for arms consists of two lines at the ends of which the hands are symbolically represented by three radial strokes. But, as further investigations will again show, we cannot speak of a general rule for the formation of these representative symbols in so far as the same representative can change according to the emphasis placed on it by the child. Further we find in the inflexible schema for the arm a line with five radial strokes or three to five transversal strokes for fingers, or the hand represented as a transversal stroke with lines radiating from it, a circle to represent the hand with an indefinite number of radial finger strokes, and, finally, for the arm, a double line that widens to form the hand and ends in ellipses for the fingers.

The representation of legs and feet also varies widely and their development follows much the same lines we have discussed in the case of the arms. The most important signs for legs and feet are two simple strokes ; double lines closed at the bottom ; single lines with a small circle at the end which occasionally is indented to show the heel ; and straight or bent double lines ending in a pediform projection.

At first, the legs and arms are frequently attached to the head. Often the arms are joined to the single or double line representing the neck. Any arbitrary portion of the body may serve as a starting point for the arm. But here, too, I must emphasise that these starting points can be enumerated in this way only for the inflexible schema. It is only after a schema has been created for the body that we can say of the starting places for the legs that they are now closer together and now further apart.

This brief description of schematic forms for normal sighted children may be followed up in greater detail in the works of Levinstein, Kerschensteiner, and Sully. We shall leave the description at this point, as we are concerned with a rather more restricted phenomenological point of view.

(2) *The First Deviation of the Schema on the Basis of the Autoplastic Experience of Form*

If we accept the inflexible schema as an *a priori* datum in infantile drawings, every deviation from it will have to be investigated according to its origin and its meaning. In what follows we shall consider autoplastic creations as the vehicle of expression in the artistic efforts of weak sighted children.

Fig. 10 is described by D. H. (Table II, No. 3) as follows : " Someone is barked at by a dog, who is on a chain. He is very frightened and wants to run away, but he is so frightened that he can't start." After a pause : " You know, that happened to me once." Fig. 10, " Man with a Bag," shows the inflexible schema which he usually employs in depicting a man and the deviations from it give us clear insight into his experience. The most remarkable thing in Fig. 10 is the new symbol for ' hand '. In the case of the inflexible schema this is merely a line with five radial strokes. But in the expressive drawing the hand becomes a circle with the fingers radiating from it in the shape of a star. We note further that in shading both the dog and the hands black—normally he does not use shading—he apparently wished to establish a relation between the two. The new symbol for the hand, these rigid, stretched fingers, record the strong autoplastic manifestation of fear. In the inflexible schema D. H. represents the legs with two simple lines, but in fig. 10 they have become double lines. His fright and desire to run away has made him more intensely conscious of his legs and so he has changed the representation of the legs and in addition given them a special movement. We may note also that the feet, which are represented in the inflexible schema, have been left out in the expressive drawing and we may perhaps see in this an attempt to indicate that he is unable to run away. In the inflexible schema the body is straight but here it has been bent and again indicates the autoplastic experience of being jerked back by fright.

In fig. 11 G. R. draws herself as having a headache. Another person is comforting her. Notice that the intensified awareness of the head because of the pain is represented by over-emphasis in the drawing. In this case it is not the schema which has been altered, but merely the size of one part, so as to indicate its special importance. Fig. 12 is a drawing on the same theme by D. H. " I have such a head-ache that I can hardly stand," he says. The strongly over-emphasised head which has to be supported by the arm is allowed to fall over sideways. Not being able to stand is expressed by giving the legs double lines instead of the more usual single lines.

The three drawings by L. B., figs. 13, 14, and 15, show the earliest manifestation of autoplastic drawing. Fig. 13 is his inflexible schema for a man. Fig. 14 represents two children running after each other in the game of ' captures '. At this early stage of his development L. B. is not able to express movement. He therefore transforms the movement which he experiences in himself into an over-emphasis of the length of the legs. If we compare this with his inflexible schema we also notice, that in addition to the length of the legs, the feet and the hands have been emphasised. The inflexible schema represents the mouth by only one line. But in the one who is doing the catching it is represented as a line with strokes across it for teeth. " You know, when I run very fast I press my teeth together," he says, and so explains the changes that come over the mouth. In the inflexible schema the arms consist of a single line whereas in fig. 14 the palm and the fingers are shown. This clearly represents the importance they have for catching.

Fig. 15 represents " someone who is thinking very hard and supporting his head in his hands ". " Thinking hard " is represented by over-emphasising the head. Comparing this drawing with the inflexible schema we see that he has left out the mouth. This *omission* of the representative symbol is quite intelligible if we think of our bodily sensations. When we are thinking hard the mouth disappears from our consciousness of the body. Looking more closely at the arm and hand on which the head is leaning, we see that the latter is entirely detached from the body. Knowing the origin of the drawing we can now quite clearly understand the formative intention expressed in it. He first drew the hand that supports the head and then continued the broken line to the table without connecting it to the body. Through the support of the elbow on the table it has lost the feeling of being connected with the body. If the reader will try this out for himself he will at once see how completely convincing this explanation is.

Fig. 8 is a further example of autoplastic drawing by D. H. " This one is catching the other. He grabs and seizes him. Hooray ! Now he's got him ! " His intense bodily sensations are characterised by the enormous length of the grasping arms with the specially emphasised clutching fingers. The double line of the legs as contrasted with the single line to be found in the inflexible schema again emphasises the special importance of these limbs in this particular theme. A further fact of importance is pointed out by D. himself who says, pointing to the shorter legs of the first figure, " Look ! he can't run so quickly. That is why he is caught." In other words slower running is represented by shorter legs. In addition he omits the arms of the captive entirely. This on the one hand expresses visibly the unimportance of the arms, and on the other the fact that they are not a part of his emotional experience.

A particularly interesting piece of work that displays a new type of autoplastic drawing is shown in fig. 16, again by D. H., " Searching for the Lost Pencil." In this picture the arms and hands are the vehicles of expression and by means of them four phases of the theme are symbolised. The intense experience of searching and of groping about after something indefinite is expressed on the one hand by the different emphasis and exaggeration of the arm, and on the other by changes in the shape of the hand. The enormously lengthened groping arm shows how the representation of the hand has been modified by the experience of clutching. " With this hand he has just found the pencil," he says, pointing to the other hand holding the pencil. The arm still shows a double line indicating its special functional importance. The hand, however, is now less emphasised because the experience of clutching is no longer the dominant one. Notice particularly the pencil. It is the Braille pencil with which the blind write and is enormously exaggerated. " With *this* hand he puts it in his pocket," he says and points to one of the arms of the second figure, which represents the same figure as the first one. In other words he has represented four temporal phases by means of two figures. He might just as well have given one figure four arms ; but this would have contradicted his experience. The arm which is putting the pencil into the pocket is now far less emphasised and is represented by a single line only whilst the second arm of the figure, having no longer a function, has shrivelled to a mere stump. Bending down and standing upright are represented by means of differences in the length of the legs. It would be difficult to find a drawing which more clearly shows in a single picture the exaggerated importance of the sensations in the arms which force the child to modify its inflexible schema. By means of this drawing we can illustrate still another experience originating in bodily sensations. According to D. the left figure is supposed to be bent forward. This is expressed by means of shorter legs and a lowered head.   The other figure on the right is standing upright whilst pocketing the pencil and this is expressed by longer legs and an upright head.   But when the head is bent forward we become more intensely aware of it because the blood accumulates in it.   This is expressed in the drawing by an exaggeration of the size of the bent head.

Out of the wealth of material at my disposal I present the following because in their different ways they again illustrate the importance of autoplastic elements in the drawings of children.   Fig. 17 shows G. R. looking at her presents.   A comparison with her inflexible schema (fig. 11) shows in what way this drawing deviates.   Two new representative symbols have appeared for the cheeks.[1]   They must therefore have entered in some way into her experience.   A study of their arrangement will lead us on the right lines.   We see that they have been drawn asymmetrically and that this asymmetry also appears in the lines for the head.   In fact the lines for the two cheeks intersect.   Now gazing at her presents was the occasion for this drawing and we must therefore seek in this experience some explanation for the displacement of the two halves of the face.   The distortion in fact corresponds to the autoplastic experience of the way in which G. R. is forced to look at things.   Because she is extremely weak sighted she has to bring things, at which she wishes to look, very close to her eyes, so closely that even her nose gets into the way.   Consequently she can only see a thing with one eye and this effort of looking sideways is represented by the asymmetry in the drawing.

This discussion leads us to consider the representation of mimicry and gesture.   Kerschensteiner maintains that it is quite immaterial for the modes of expression of a child " whether it draws a snowball fight or a funeral procession. The human schema always remains the same ".   The course of our investigation so far has shown the schema to be modifiable and should therefore have convinced us that schematic representations are influenced by numerous circumstances. We must now investigate how far the child possesses the

[1] W. Stern in *Psychology of Early Childhood* has also noted that his son drew separate representative symbols for cheeks.

ability to represent gestures within the limits of its schema.

Fig. 18 shows the most primitive stage of such an 'expressive mask'. It shows a man yawning. When the child made this drawing it was at what we have called the pre-schematic executive stage. The child had not yet found a relatively permanent form of expressing itself by means of a schema. This, then, is one of the earliest ways in which facial expression and movement are depicted. We can feel the power of primitive art here more clearly than in almost any other primitive representation. To begin with we see no more than a meaningless mass of lines. But if we have the strength of mind to subordinate our personality to the work, we see it suddenly as the vehicle of elemental sensations derived from facial expression. The two horizontal lines become the boundaries of the wide open jaws stretching across the whole width of the head. The teeth are expressed by means of small strokes and so serve to give plastic shape to the cavity of the mouth. When we realise that the two circles to the right and left below the mouth represent ears we recognise that in the muscular sensations of yawning the ears are included. If the reader will try it out for himself he will be better able to understand how here for the first time these elemental forces emerge into clear expression. The eyes and the nose are drawn alike and have meaning only because of their location. We have here, then, the first formal representation of the experience of a facial expression. Fig. 19, which depicts the same subject, belongs to the same executive stage. Here yawning is expressed by the wide open mouth and intensified by the skew outline of the head while all other representative symbols have been omitted. Figs. 20 and 21 represent a slightly higher stage of development. In fig. 20 by K. W. (Table II, No. 5) we see how the chin (K.), throat (H.) and chest (B.) are drawn into the circumference of the expressive mask corresponding to the bodily experience of the artist. In fig. 21 those parts which are experienced with especial intensity have been left white. But we shall see that later on the gradually increasing schematism also stereotyped this particular way of drawing.

I told the children a story in which there was an accident that made one of the heroes of the story very sad and the other cheerful. I then asked them to draw these two heroes. In almost all cases the schema remained the same, but the sad person was in general enlarged (fig. 22). For lack of a greater number of experiments I can do no more than venture the hypothesis that our self-consciousness appears intensified in pain and that this enlargement of the schema is an indication of intensified autoplastic experience. At all events I have found that drawing facial expressions and gestures is not only not predominant during the schematic stage of development but seems almost impossible. The reasons for this seem to me to be on the one hand the low flexibility of the individual schematic representative symbols through which the expressions are depicted, and on the other a low capacity for co-ordination which hinders the child from drawing expressions. The child draws the representative symbol as such without considering its effect in relation to the other vehicles of expression. I have frequently observed that children call this or that product " a man crying " or " a man laughing " although it is hardly possible to see any difference in the drawings. " Daddy, look! he is crying," my son said to me once, pointing to a drawing which he had just made. He pointed to a slightly enlarged line representing the mouth. Looking at his numerous drawings no one would be able to spot this one as " a man crying ". But obviously the intention was present when the child was making the drawing. It seems clear therefore that it is *our* incapacity to see that prevents us from appreciating the meaning of changes in the schema. We are far too prone to recognize only that which immediately manifests its meaning to our visual perception. If, for instance, crying were to be represented by a new form for tears we should have no difficulty in perceiving it (fig. 23). But can we draw from this the conclusions which Kerschensteiner drew ?

The work of A. (fig. 24) also does not fall entirely into the class of autoplastic drawings. " Someone is shaking the nut tree in the garden." To represent shaking the tree the schema has been modified by exaggerating the arms. But what is important here is that the force exerted in shaking the tree is represented by placing the man at an angle and this angle has become decisive for the pictorial relationship of tree and man. I have observed this case only once but mention it because it finds a parallel in the work of Voss.[1] Voss, however, maintains that this form of expression is generally to be found in the drawings of blind people.

The cases we have discussed, which were chosen as characteristic examples out of a great mass of material, show clearly that changes and exaggerations of the symbols for form and expression as well as innovations of individual representative symbols take place on the basis of autoplastic experience. The formal symbols are omitted whenever this corresponds to experience. Furthermore we have seen that the representation of facial expression and gesture has its earliest beginnings in states of autoplastic experience. The schema therefore has developed from these bodily experiences and we may conclude that *the autoplastic experience of form shown in the drawings of children who are weak sighted is of the greatest importance for creative expression.*

(3) *The Over-emphasis of Meaningful Parts*

Another kind of change in the proportions of children's drawings springs from the tendency to exaggerate the size of objects having a special significance. Some examples follow to illustrate this creative principle.

K. was chosen to light the candlesticks at a party. Fig. 25, by K. W., shows this scene. We at once notice the enormous candlestick compared with the small figure. This disproportion arises because in the experience the candlestick predominated. When talking about his drawing he said, "You see, I stretch my arms through these branches till I come to the middle candle." This was not, of course, what actually happened. But his uncertainty in carrying out an action to which he was not accustomed is expressed by the feeling that he had to grope his way. This explains the over-emphasised arm with the strokes for fingers, which in his

[1] Voss, W., "Subjektive und objektive Aufbauelemente in den Zeichnungen Blinder."

inflexible schema appear as a simple line. The other arm, having no function, was simply omitted.

Fig. 26 by L. B. shows a rider sitting on a horse that is being pestered by flies. L. draws one fly almost as large as the horse and this shows that in the experience that preceded the drawing it was not the horse but the bothersome flies that seemed of the greatest importance. Indeed the head of the horse is merely represented by two circles for the eyes and another circle for the mouth, whereas the tail— " he is waving his tail "—is clearly characterised.

D. H. draws someone looking out of a window (fig. 27). To the left and right of him there is a cupboard and further to the right a table with a small stick. In the ' background ' stands a bed. The outer limits of the drawing also indicate the limits of the room. In this way we can understand the bed in the background. He is here confusing plan and front elevation. The strong exaggeration of the size of the figure indicates the theme of the drawing. Whereas the cupboard, table and stick and also the bed are represented in the proper proportions to one another, the window with the figure and in particular the head are strongly over-emphasised. This shows that when no particular aspect is important, size relationships are objectively represented whilst the subjective experience is not subordinated to these general laws of proportion. Only when we look at a drawing in this way can we understand the *intention* behind the drawing.

Fig. 28 by D. H. shows two chess players. The tables, the chairs, and the players are drawn in front elevation, but the chess board is drawn in plan. By this change of aspect he immediately emphasises the importance of the game of chess.

Fig. 29 shows K. W. receiving his birthday presents. On the left is a small case, in the middle a calculating machine, and on the right a radio set. On the floor is a railway. He himself is drawn quite small, almost at the edge. The important things in this drawing are the presents. Moreover, when he was drawing the table for the radio he said, " You know, of course, the radio is very heavy " and for this reason he changed the representative symbol for table top by making it much thicker.

K. W. drew a dog hanging on a chain and barking (fig. 30). " You know, I am very much afraid of such dogs but this one, you see, is on a *strong* chain." Consequently, the individual links of the chain are the biggest and most important things in this drawing.

These few but typical examples show that the infantile drawings of the weak sighted are replete with valuations. The relations between objects are relations of value and it is only when we perceive this important principle that the drawings become intelligible. The child draws ' objective proportions ' of objects only when he stands in no special relation to them. We are therefore compelled to recognize that *proportions, and in many cases also changes in representative symbols, are to the widest possible degree dependent on the subjective attitudes called out by an experience.*

(4) *The Importance of Value Judgments in Infantile Drawings*

As soon as we recognize that values are important in the art of children, subjective experience automatically becomes the central point for our consideration of the art of children. We have shown that disproportions nearly always result from some definite intention though this intention is not necessarily conscious. We therefore no longer have the right to speak of ' false proportions ' since such a judgment is determined by our visual attitude, the attitude of ' objective experience of the environment '. On the contrary, it is only when we understand the reasons for these apparent disproportions that we are able to penetrate into the true roots of creativeness. *Naturalistic tendencies and conceptions, therefore, are totally unsuitable means for the understanding of children's drawings.* The child is intimately bound up with the experience of the self and experiences its world subjectively. Although such executive intentions have frequently been recognized, they have not been given their proper place in the treatment of children's drawings.

Bühler says, " one of the most important generalizations

about children's drawings is that articulation is equivalent to a separation into component parts, which, contrary to the whole spirit of painting, is the order of knowledge." It is probably true to say that there is some such " order of knowledge ", but this is in all probability not particularly characteristic of the drawings of children because the child frequently does not draw things which it knows about. No one will doubt that a child *knows* that a man has two arms ; yet, as we have shown, these are sometimes omitted. But it is important to note that in such a case the determinants underlying such an omission are in strong contradiction to the ' conceptual ' drawing and thought of the child. If we interpret Bühler's statement to the effect that this order of knowledge corresponds to the degree of experience his statement would be more valid. When discussing the question of ' order ' Bühler says that the child frequently draws in the same irregular order in which it enumerates objects. " The horse has a head and tail, two legs in front and at the back also two. . . ." [1] This way of counting things, Bühler thinks, may account for the unordered form of presentation that does not allow the child to bring the head and the tail into the proper relation with the limbs. But this is not so. The child will think of a horse in this unordered fashion only if the adult forces it to think of ' a horse ' as such. If on the other hand it thinks of an experience it has had in connection with a horse then a *definite order is introduced into this disordered thinking by the intensity of the experience*. Naturally this order does not arise out of visual experience but is an order of values. Bühler's conclusion that " the child lacks an embracing and critically ordered spatial imagination " is therefore quite true ; but for this particular ' lapse ' he has substituted an *order of values*. To return to our original example (fig. 26) : the child does not think in the way Bühler imagines, but, " a fly comes along " (starting point of the experience) " and lands on the horse. The horse wags its tail and tries to drive away the irritating fly ". So it draws the overlarge fly and the tail which is waving and nothing more. The fact that the horse has legs is already

[1] Bühler, K., *Mental Development of the Child*, Kegan Paul, 1931.

part of its schema. Consequently they are drawn in the manner demanded by this particular symbol, that is, without reference to reality and without experiencing anew a directive concept of order. In the earliest drawings of children we can observe this order that springs from experience and relates things according to their value. It is, of course, true that this order is eminently abstract.

W. Stern also emphasises the non-visual attitude of the child towards its drawings. " Not only are all æsthetic intentions originally absent but even the tendency to reproduce actually visible objects." Stern further observes that a four year old child knows perfectly well that human beings have ears, " but it does not always remember to actualise this knowledge in a drawing and in the finished drawing it does not miss the part that is lacking." This leaves unanswered two questions : *when* does the child not actualise its knowledge while drawing, and *why* does it not feel the lack of a missing part in the finished drawing ?

Although Wulff recognizes that " at the earliest ages proportions depend on the tension between two contradictory forces : concepts on the one hand and the tendency to movement on the other ", and that therefore " as long as no exact image of the whole is present during drawing every part will have its value emphasised by size ", he apparently denies this later. For, speaking of the progressive development towards realistic representation, he says, " occasional distortions are still found. Thus the neck is occasionally left out although a month previously the correct starting point for the arms had been tried out on two female busts, and in the second the neck had been properly drawn." " The arms also are frequently drawn either too long or unequal and the feet too large." [1]

These quotations illustrate very clearly that there are still far too many naturalistic attitudes hampering the investigation of the psychology of children's art. My investigations have shown that the child does not fall a

[1] Wulff is here referring to fig. 40 in his *Die Kunst des Kindes*. It shows a man with a walking stick. His hand, because it carries the stick, is enlarged. As he is concerned with realistic proportions, Wulff quite overlooks the fact that the disproportion is caused by attention to the relevant experience.

prey to an inflexible schema but, using its own individual experience, it creatively transforms the schema in the act of creation.

(e) THE DEVELOPMENT OF SPATIAL PHENOMENA

When we speak of the representation of space in children's drawings we can only mean its symbolic and not its naturalistic representation. When the child represents space it uses lines to symbolise at one time the base on which things stand and at another the character of the landscape. It mixes together plan and front elevation and in this way creates its own concept of space. But these are not the only modes of projection. Objects in a plane are ' folded over ' and in this way the child creates a type of space which seems to us to be a construct and reminds us of the methods of projective geometry. In every case the representation of space by the child is symbolic and extremely abstract. If we are going to speak of a *development* in the representation of space, we must be quite clear that the childish representations of space are only uniform when space is represented in such a way that the child is not itself so involved in the experience of space that subjective experience and space become a unity. In other words, if a room or landscape is represented as such, if there is nothing that has directly influenced the child, then one can speak of *objective space*.

The development of objective space may very broadly be considered as a *development towards as well as away from a ' base line.'* This means that in the confusion of the earliest drawings of children the base line gradually becomes the co-ordinating factor that not only fixes the standpoint but also indicates direction within the general spatial arrangement. Order resulting from the criterion of importance plays no part in objective space because it is a subjective measure involving the self. This is what I mean by development towards the base line. And by development away from the base line I mean that as the process of ' visual perceiving ' develops, the plane is more and more recognized as a unity, so that, through the development of perspective, the base line is gradually displaced by the plane. Wulff maintains that the

E

omission of the base line rests on the simple optical perception that the ground lying in front of our feet seems to rise. " In this way ' over each other ' becomes ' behind each other '." It is only when space perception has developed that the base *line* looses its symbolic nature and makes way for the unified *plane*.

Parallel to this development, however, we can observe another in which the base line permanently remains the symbolic vehicle of a fictitious representation of space. To this group belong the well-known strip pictures in which ' space ' is depicted by a number of base lines arranged above one another so that the picture is divided into plane strips.

In both cases, however, when the experience of the child is directly involved in the representation of spatial objects and not merely objects as such are being represented, then objects are grouped in ' space ' according to the intensity of the experience. Grouping takes place according to subjective and not according to universally valid points of view. In that case I use the term *subjective space* or *ego-bound space*.

(1) *Objective Space*

Fig. 31 represents the earliest schematic representation of objective space (L. B., Table II, No. 2). It depicts a street. The line upon which trees as well as human beings are standing represents therefore not only the base line on which the objects represented stand but the street itself. We cannot, of course, assume that the child knew nothing about the width or other properties of the street. The line is merely a symbol for everything connected with ' street '. In a later picture we see the same child consciously drawing both sides of the street (fig. 32). But we must not imagine that the two base lines represent the lateral boundaries of the street, that is that the space between the two lines represents the surface of the street. The two sides are purely conceptual formulations and the drawing is nothing more than the representation of one street at the top and one at the bottom, that is, a repetition of the first picture. By means of this repetition the double sidedness of the street is conceptually indicated and expressed merely symbolically.

That this is so is quite clear from the fact that vehicles have been drawn on *both* base lines.   Similarly, a superficial examination of fig. 33 might lead one to believe that this represents a *view* of a street since one might think that the two people walking must be walking on the two pavements. In point of fact the mode of representation in this figure is the same as in fig. 32.

A different mode of presenting a street is shown in fig. 34 *a* and *b*. Here again the base line represents at one and the same time the base for the houses and trees as well as the street itself. The mode of representation is therefore analogous to that of fig. 32, except that here the fact that there are two rows of houses has been indicated by ' folding over ' one of the rows. We observe further that both L. B. and K. W. keep to this schema for ' street '. It is abandoned only when subjective grounds of experience demand a different method of representation, as for example in fig. 34*b*, in which K. wishes to express that he heard a newspaper vendor on the other side of the street. The two lines enclosing the street here do not correspond to the developmental phase of fig. 32—the double sidedness has already been expressed by folding over—but indicate the subjective feeling of distance which in this drawing was for him the significant experience. This assertion is made convincing by the fact that in all his future drawings of the street he returns to the schema of fig. 34. The same spatial schema is expressed by G. R. in fig. 35, " A girl picking flowers." The meadow is indicated by a base line. This base line also stands for the earth and symbolises not only the ground out of which the grasses grow but the extension of the whole surface. By ' folding over ' one of the rows of the meadows, G. wished to indicate " that the flowers grow everywhere " and expressively illustrated the experience that when picking flowers you could grasp them on all sides.

Again, whenever the child wishes to depict *direction*, the base line is used to express this direction. Figs. 36 and 37 show a road with trees which leads to a rondeau. Fig. 36 shows the road in the manner described above. The base line represents the street and on it on both sides grow the trees. In the drawing these have been ' folded over '. Where the rondeau is situated, the base line describes a circle to characterise it. It might be thought that the rondeau is here depicted in plan and that this is the intention of the circle, but the drawing shows clearly that the *area* of the circle has no meaning, that is, has not been intended by the child. The width of the street, that is its surface area, is not depicted any more than the circular area of the rondeau. If the circle had a specific meaning for the child, it would have drawn the street in its proper width where it ends in the rondeau. But the street is depicted in its characteristic linear extension just as the rondeau in its circular extension. In other words the base line here also determines the direction. The trees grow vertically out of the base line corresponding to trees growing out of the soil. Fig. 37 might lead us to believe that a different intention underlies this drawing since we see here that the street and the rondeau were *apparently* depicted as planes. But the linear connection between rondeau and street shows that this is not so. Here, too, the base line is merely a base for the trees. We are simply dealing with another schema for expressing the concept of two rows. The line connecting the street and the rondeau has a merely conceptual character : it establishes the unity between the two. The child first drew the street and then somewhere else the rondeau ; but since the street was supposed to lead into the rondeau a line connecting the two was put in afterwards.

Figs. 38 and 39 can now be considered quite briefly. Fig. 38 shows a street which goes around a block of houses. Fig. 39 shows a square surrounded by houses. The two pictures reveal that the houses are folded inwards or folded outwards according to the particular pictorial intention. In fig. 38 the street which leads around the block of houses is the starting point of the representation. Consequently, in the picture the street runs round the houses and acts both as a baseline for the houses and as a frame. I asked a child to draw a courtyard surrounded by houses. The result was the same as in fig. 39, which represents a square. Thus it is the square which is emphasised and the houses are therefore folded over outwards.   Again the boundary of the square is the base line for the houses.   We see that the houses are folded over vertically because they must stand vertically on their base.   In other words, *the pictorial intention determines the direction in which objects are ' folded over '*.

We shall conclude our observations of these representations of level country with fig. 40, which depicts a park. K. draws a park in which a man carrying flowers is taking a walk on one of the paths. Again we are dealing with purely linear representation. The frame is formed by the fence which is drawn as folded over perpendicular to its base line. Here, too, the rectangular space included by the fence has not been conceived as a plane, the base line merely representing the conceived boundary of the park.   Two paths lead diagonally through the park. Both act as base lines for the trees as well as for the walker. This is quite clear when we consider their relative positions.   " The walker is going along one side of the path, the trees stand on the other." This remark of K.'s clearly shows the double meaning of the base line as a path with two sides and as a basis for trees and walker. He says further, " you see, the tree, just like ours, is growing over the fence." This remark was made after the picture had been finished. In other words it does not express an original intention but shows that the space between the trees has no particular meaning. K. remembers that the tree grows upwards over the fence. The configuration of the ground, however, is regarded as being identical with that of the base line. Consequently he has folded over the trees perpendicularly in order to indicate that " the trees grow upwards ". This symbolic meaning of the base lines shows us that the spaces between them are not intended to have a meaning of their own.

We now proceed to the representation of a surface which is not plane. Fig. 41 shows two people who are climbing a mountain. In the drawing they are proceeding from right to left. But for us the base line seems to contradict this as it seems to be going down hill. This shows that, at this particular stage, L. does not represent the concept ' hill ' by the upward wending line to which we adults are accustomed. Up and down as intentions of direction have not yet been fixed. The hill itself, however, has been rendered by means of the very much strengthened base line which for him evidently expresses the meaning of the concept ' hill '. Thus to indicate ' climbing ', it is sufficient for him to bring the persons into direct relation with his symbol for ' hill ' and to place the two figures on this thickened line which expresses ' hill '. These pictures show that where the child has not yet found modes of expressing in a form which corresponds to his personal experience, things perceivable by the senses, he introduces a sign which, though it has no direct relation with reality, nevertheless expresses the intention underlying his drawing.

Fig. 42 is an extremely interesting picture of a small house on a mountain. As in the previous example this does not yet represent a final stage in the sense of being a schema. Here, too, the immediate configuration of ' space ' starts from the base line (a). At first this was not drawn as long as it finally appears. It went only from (b) to (c). In other words it was meant to represent the peak of the mountain. From here G. drew lines in such a way that, as she said, " you can see how one could go down from the mountain." She added, " You see, that is how I would model a mountain." This indicates the immediate physical experience of climbing down a mountain, or as in the case of modelling, of the gliding down of the fingers. The lines are similar to contour lines on a map and like these indicate the gradient. The house was meant to stand at the top of the mountain. Consequently, the line b–c representing the peak was lengthened so that it could also serve as the base line for the house. In this way the base line of the house was brought into direct relationship to the peak to show that the two belonged together. When I asked where the trees stood, G. answered, " on both sides of the mountain." So the folding over of the trees is explained by her answer.

If, however, climbing up the mountain has been perceived sensorially (visually or kinæsthetically) and brought into harmony with the base line, then we get a representation of a mountain such as we are accustomed to see and as is shown in fig. 43. Here on a base line symbolising the plain, another base line is drawn to represent the mountain.[1] In other words the child wishes to indicate that this base line is elevated over the plain and it represents the surface character of the landscape. But we can see from the fact that the trees stand perpendicularly to the ' mountain ', that here, too, the growing upwards of the trees is bound to a base line. This is even more characteristically expressed in fig. 44, in which the house is drawn perpendicularly to the mountain. We can only understand this when we perceive that the line bou·.ding the mountain becomes the base line for the house and it is from this base line that the house is built vertically upwards. The drawing shows a river over which there is a bridge (*a*). On the bridge is a man with a stick (*b*). On one side of the river is the mountain (*c*), on the other there are trees (*d*). We can see quite clearly what importance the base line has for spatial thinking in the drawings of children. The man on the bridge, the trees on the bank, the mountain in the plain, and finally the little house on the hill, all these are ordered in relation to the base line. If however, as in fig. 45, the line indicating a mountain is not intended to be a base line (the shading in figs. 45 and 46 clearly indicates the mountain to have been represented separately) then a new base line is introduced for houses and trees. The child wished to indicate a shelter on the top of a hill. D. first drew the hill using the lower edge as base line. He then shaded the hill, showing that in this case he did not intend the outline itself to have any special meaning, but the space inside it. He had created a distinct representative symbol for ' hill '. After he had so drawn the hill he drew a base line for house and trees which just touched the peak of the hill. In this way he wished to indicate that the house stood on the top. His conception, briefly, was as follows. In a plain (the lower edge of the paper also represents the plain

---

[1] Pictures like these are called ' orthoscopic ' by Bühler, and he maintains that they are one of the " preferred views ". But the way in which such drawings develop, and not merely because they are the products of weak sighted children, shows that we cannot in such cases speak of " views ".

in the form of a base line) there is a hill (representative symbol for ' hill ' : shaded triangle). On the top of the hill stands a shelter with trees. But as every house stands on a basis, and there is as yet no such basis present (the outline of the representative symbol for hill does not here function as a base line also) he had to create one. The house must stand on the hill, therefore its basis must be on the hill. Consequently the base line of the house is drawn in such a way that it touches the top of the hill and so indicates the relation between the two. Fig. 46 shows how above the shelter D. has introduced a walker climbing a lookout tower. From the base line representing the top there is a path which is drawn partly in plan and partly in front elevation leading to the lookout tower. The steps leading upwards are drawn in front elevation whilst D.'s explanation that " the path also goes *round* the lookout tower " explains its being drawn in plan. This drawing shows clearly that the representation of a hill is purely symbolic and has nothing to do with a ' view '.

Three typical drawings will illustrate how in various ways level and hilly landscapes are drawn. The subject set was : " draw a street which is at first level, then goes over a hill and then becomes level again." The children were reminded of a walk they had taken over just such a road. L. B. (fig. 47) broke his line for the level road and introduced a new symbol (A) for the hill. The relation between the road and the hill is purely symbolic. G. (fig. 48) did the same except that we can clearly see that the symbol for hill also signifies a sensory experience which we have already discussed in connection with fig. 42. He indicated the difference in level by drawing one line lower than the other. Later, the continuity of the road was established by connecting it to the ' hill '. A third mode of representation is shown in fig. 49 in which K. does not break the line for the road. But even this picture is not ' realistic '. In it the hill, like the trees, has been folded over and does not represent the incline as we would represent it. We here see clearly the opposition between subjective experience and mere conceptual knowledge. The influence of subjective experience is indicated by the continuity of the base line in spite of the intrusion of the symbolic representative for ' hill '.

The above examples show that the representation of space by the child is fictitious and that it is closely bound up with the conception of a base line. This does not merely symbolise the different dimensions but also becomes the main factor in the articulation of the picture and serves many different representational intentions. The base line is intimately bound up with the spatial representations of the weak sighted. It is a symbol of their creative work.

(2) *Subjective Space*

When objects are depicted, that feature which is characteristic or functional about the object is drawn, unless some other intention governs the mode of drawing. We shall next proceed to investigate in what way other intentions may determine the forms that are actually drawn.

Fig. 50 shows a dormitory in the school for the blind. This is one of many typical ' X-ray pictures '. The house is drawn ' transparent ', quite regardless of the front wall. This phenomenon is found frequently in the drawings of normal sighted children and has repeatedly been discussed in the literature on the subject from Ricci down to the present day. In the drawings of the weak sighted it finds a beautifully simple explanation (cf. also fig. 51).

A child blind from birth modelled a cherry as follows. First he formed its stone which he then covered with a thin skin and over this he modelled the flesh so that finally he achieved a cherry as it would appear to the touch. The stone, of course, was in the end no longer visible ; but it had been modelled because it was bound up with his conception of a cherry as closely as the inner appearance of the dormitory is bound up with D.'s conception of it when he drew fig. 50.[1] The dormitory is only part of the whole building. The upper floor was therefore also drawn to indicate this, but it was

[1] In *Plastische Arbeiten Blinder* I described how, when blind children modelled a ship, they made the engine rooms, cabins, dining saloons and so on and then covered the whole with a deck so that nothing remained to be seen of all the things inside. Nevertheless these were an inseparable part of their conception of the whole ship.

given no detail as that would have detracted from the importance of the dormitory. As the dormitory was the most important part of the drawing it was specially emphasised. The ' building as a whole ' is surrounded by a line but this line does not represent a ' house '. It merely serves as a boundary. D. next drew a line to separate off the dormitory but he did not put anything inside it. He was satisfied meanwhile with having indicated its space within the larger space. Of the line at the bottom, which also formed the base line on which the furniture stood, he said, " that is the passage ". This line, then, signifies three things.

From the line considered as passage the stairs lead to the upper storey in which the passage is again indicated by a horizontal line. We might call this an " orthoscopic representation ", to use Bühler's term. In other words, one of the " pre-eminent basic views " for steps or stairs has been drawn, or, as Jaensch would say, " it indicates the tendency to localise visual impressions perpendicularly to the line of sight." In this case, of course, we are dealing with neither the localisation of visual impressions nor with a pre-eminent basic view, as both were physically impossible. But the different way in which the stairs going up and those coming down is treated gives us a most illuminating insight into the creative activity of this little weak sighted boy. For when he had drawn the stairs going upwards as far as the passage, he drew the door. In the door he sketched some parallel lines and said, " those are the stairs that go down." He repeated the same thing in the door of the dormitory, which also shows the horizontal lines of the descending stairs quite clearly. In point of fact the steep zig-zag lines for the ascending stairs and the horizontal lines for the descending stairs represent one and the same object ; but this object, having been experienced in two different ways, is represented twice. When one goes upstairs one has a keener muscular sensation of effort and this is symbolised by the accentuated ascending stairs. Going down is much easier and therefore the lines are wider apart and horizontal. We see quite clearly how different are the experiences underlying visual and non-visual perception. In the former the *object* as such would be drawn ; in the latter the *experiences* to which the object gives rise. We shall see in what follows how deeply we can penetrate into the child's mode of creation once we have realized this difference. Let us continue to follow the time sequence of the drawings since this also seems to me important. After he had drawn the door with the descending stairs, he drew the windows of this storey without paying any particular attention to their number or order. Having now satisfied himself that he was inside the school, he turned to the drawing of the dormitory, which he again symbolised only by the objects in his immediate neighbourhood. The dormitory contains more than 20 beds ; but he drew only his own. " My bed stands close to the door " ; and that is how he drew it. Now in the dormitory all the beds are placed with their heads against the wall. It is important to remember this and we shall later see its significance. The drawing of the bed does not differ from that by a normal sighted child. It shows the lines that seem to him characteristic and also the bedside table which habitually stood next to the bed. So far the work could have been covered by the term ' orthoscopic drawing ', provided we gave it a new definition which did not include visual perception as the experience of primary importance. " Over my bedside table is a window. You see, it is closed because I often have ear-ache. The window next to it is open." He has therefore correctly shown the relation between the window and bedside table. The closed window is drawn with a cross while in the open one the cross is omitted. " That is the bedside table of B. (his neighbour)," and he draws it in the same way as his own. I shall now enumerate the order in which he drew the next set of things and give the explanation later. First he drew himself lying in bed, then the four small circles above, and finally the three objects on the neighbouring bedside table. He said, " I am lying in bed on my back and (pointing to the circles) on my left (he means on the bedside table) I always have a plate, a glass with water, a tooth mug, and a soap dish."

The insight we thus achieve into the child's mode of drawing is fascinating. D. draws himself lying on his back, that is, as seen from above, a view that conflicts with the drawing of the rest of the picture. The bed, the tables, the glasses and the soap dish on the neighbouring table are drawn in front elevation. But if D. stretches out his left hand (note that it has been overemphasised), which he probably frequently does at night, he *grasps* the objects on his bedside table. These are therefore also drawn in plan. His subjective relations to this part of space are symbolised in two ways. First, by being drawn in plan, and secondly by the fact that objects of particular importance to him are drawn quite independently of the bedside table on which they stand. The table although it carries the objects, is quite unimportant ; it is the subjective experience of the sense of touch which predominates. The space which has been represented, therefore, is independent of reality and the relationships within it are subjective. This space I shall call *affective space*. How different the two spaces are we see immediately if we compare the ' correct ' proportions of the glasses and dishes drawn in front elevation on his neighbour's bedside table, with the greatly exaggerated circles he drew to represent the same sort of objects on his own table. It is interesting to note that some time elapsed between the drawing of the circles on his left and the drawing of the glasses on the bedside table of his neighbour. Apparently the thought came to him that B., his neighbour, must also have glasses and a soap dish on his table ; so he drew these as well. But since the intention underlying the drawing of these was determined purely by objective facts, he chose to represent them orthoscopic.

This drawing, then, shows particularly plainly what I understand by affective space. But it is to be found some-where or other in almost every child's pictures. In what follows we shall consider a few typical examples in order to discover the way in which subjective experience deter-mines the presentation of forms and of space, and to see how far we can deduce this experience of the child from such changes in shape.

Fig. 52 shows a drawing by A. entitled " Saying Good-bye ". The intentions underlying the drawing are similar to the ones discussed above but there are certain peculiarities which merit a closer scrutiny. A. is sitting in the carriage. " The guard has already closed the door and is giving the signal for the train to go off." Note the overemphasised arm. " I quickly shake hands with my father. He cries. Now the train is off." It is remarkable that A. is apparently not sitting in the carriage but lying down although sitting could have been better and more characteristically expressed by the usual side view drawn in elevation (cf. fig. 28d). A, however, has chosen to draw in plan. As he has drawn the carriage in the same projection he must have had some special intention and this is made clear by his further explanation. Pointing to the two figures of his father and the guard, he says, " You see, they stand." He drew a number of vertical lines in the air to make himself plain, " and," waving his pencil about horizontally, " I am riding." In other words, by drawing the carriage and everything connected with himself in *plan* and his father and the guard in *elevation*, he has indicated that remaining behind is static in contrast to the dynamic aspect of riding away. We can now clearly understand the difference between a vertical line which is bound to its base and is finite, and the floating, infinite horizontal line ; and we may be reminded of similarly significant aspects in the composition of great works of art.

The following experience underlies fig. 53. One summer K. lived in a house not far from a hill. From this house two paths led up the hill, at the top of which there was a shelter. K. and a friend decided to climb by different paths and to meet at the shelter. First K. drew the hill with the shelter. " The hill has two depressions " and while he was drawing he showed me how he left the depressions empty and filled in the rest of the hill in black. Here it is the empty space which is significant, in contrast to the empty space between the paths and the hill, which has no significance. He now drew the paths and said at once where the house was to be, " you see, that is where I am going to put the house," and then drew the long curve downwards. He next drew the house and it should be noted that the upward tendency of both hill and house have become determinants of direction in his drawing. Both are drawn *upwards*. The ' road ' provided a base line for the house, but for the ' hill ' he introduced a new one. K. stopped drawing and said, " now both of us, I and my friend, come *out* of the house." While saying this he turned the paper through 180°. " I am going the longer way and he the shorter. Now I have come to a tree." He drew the tree. With his eyes he ' felt ' his way further down the path. When he came to the curve he again turned the paper through 180°. " There you are, I am already at the top ! " He drew himself. He repeated the process on the other side when drawing his friend. In other words K. represented his going out by turning the paper through 180°. If he had drawn the figure immediately after it had come out of the house, it would simply have been ' folded over '. This is clear from the way in which he has depicted the trees, that in a quasi symbolic manner, are designed to indicate how he and his friend went. As he has related these trees to himself, " I come to a tree," he has drawn them just as he would have drawn himself. His subjective experience, then, determined this particular way of drawing.

From other drawings we can see how *order* could be brought into a drawing only through intensive *personal experience*. In fig. 54, D. wished to draw a boy on a sledge who is propelling himself by means of ' oars '. (' Oars ' are what the blind call two sticks by means of which they push the sledge along in the level snow. By pushing the sticks into the snow at the back they propel themselves forward.) Fig. 54*a* shows that D. was unable to relate the sledge to the man. When I told him to think of the effort required for ' rowing ' he drew 54*b* and explained it as follows : " Do you see now what an effort he is making ? He is bending forward and pushing hard ! See how he is pressing his teeth together ! " Because of the sensation arising when the teeth are pressed firmly together the head has been much overemphasised. At the same time, however, this heightened consciousness of the body also brings order into the spatial representation. D. feels that his feet are on the runners and therefore brings them into the correct relation to the sledge.

To sum up : subjective space can always be perceived wherever personal experience stands at the centre of the creative act and thus becomes a measure of the value of all those things which surround a particular experience. Moreover the forms which through it have received an expressive content are frequently separated from the rest of the drawing, which is merely schematic, and lead us directly to the true source of the experience.

(f) SPACE AND TIME IN DRAWINGS

Just as the child has its own way of depicting two and three dimensional objects according to its experiences, so it has its own way of depicting events that have several phases in time. We may compare the drawing of temporal events with the child's drawings in which plan and elevation and X-ray pictures are mingled. Just as different spatial ' views ' are fused in the conceptions of the child, so ' views ' that are separated in time also fuse to a unity in the child's conceptions. But their psychological origin is often somewhat different. Levinstein [1] distinguishes three ways of telling a story, the ' narrative ', the ' fragmentary ', and between these the ' continuous '.[2] He gives examples of all three kinds in the children's drawings illustrated in his book. By examining some characteristic drawings of weak sighted children we shall now attempt to investigate somewhat more closely the problems of form that arise.

The drawings in which the temporal sequence of actions is depicted have two different psychological roots, to each of which there corresponds an adequate formal representation. The child likes to hear as well as to tell stories. One manner of creating forms arises out of this need for communication. So we find different episodes represented by different

---

[1] S. Levinstein, *Kinderzeichnungen bis zum* 14. *Lebensjahr*, Leipzig.

[2] In his book *Die Wiener Genesis* Wickhoff distinguishes three ways of telling a story which are very similar to those of Levinstein. The ' distinguishing ' (Levinstein's ' narrative ') type places side by side specially selected themes either in isolation or connected by a mere framework. In the ' continuous ' story actions that are separated in space or in time are represented by means of the principle of repetition ; and the ' complementary ' (Levinstein's ' fragmentary ') type attempts to represent everything that happens before or afterwards and seems important for the action, without repeating the actors.

pictures in the same drawing. The pictures are separate and it is of no significance whether the individual theme really has been divided by a line or whether the division is purely fictitious. It is characteristic of this ' narrative ' representation that the action as a whole is drawn repeatedly, often with different surroundings. Fig. 55 is a typical example. The subject depicted here by K. is " Off for the Summer ". On the left at the bottom he shows how the trunk is packed. Then he draws the street showing us the way to the station. It is a street lined with trees through which he and his friend have to go. Finally, in the top left hand corner he describes the departure. "Do you see how we have to wait on the platform ? We are already quite trembly with excitement." He points to the zig-zag line of the ' hands ' by means of which this is depicted. " And now we have got in." (This is symbolised by the black shading in the ' train '.) " Now we are off." He inserts the engine and the smoke. He is thus describing a complex event and the form which he chooses is that of separate pictures whose relation to each other is one of content. The second picture, in which temporally distinct actions are represented in one space, is somewhat different. It does not spring from the desire to communicate something and its origin must be sought in the act of drawing itself. The importance of the action diminishes the child's consciousness of time to such an extent that it is not aware of representing phases differing in time. It is only concerned with expressing within one drawing what it regards as most characteristic about the action, in much the same way as alternations between plan and elevation are used to express what is most characteristic about an object. In the one case temporally distinct phases, in the other spatially distinct impressions are used for characterization. It is important to realise that in this type of picture the drawing is confined to a single sequence of actions or movements and that placing the various aspects next to each other in one ' space ' is employed merely as a method of characterization. I have found that in the work of the weak sighted this type of drawing is more frequent than the ' narrative ' type. I believe that this is owing to the more intimate experience of the self that the weak sighted child has.

As a typical and also as the simplest example of this type of drawing we may take fig. 56 by D., " a Football Player," in which we can see the phenomenon twice. By representing the football twice D. wished to express the characteristic flight of the ball and this is made clearer still by connecting the two drawings of the ball with a line. But in this connection the second phenomenon seems to me even more important. On the figure on the left he drew the nose in profile and then added a second nose, saying, " he is just turning round." This means that he first looked to the left and then as soon as the ball came he turned round. If the child had thought of the player as looking towards the right from the beginning he would naturally have drawn a right handed profile. (Cf. fig. 60.) Thus it was the *movement* which he wished to express. Therefore he characterised it by drawing two noses, and as soon as the second nose was drawn the first lost its significance.

Another characteristic example is to be found in fig. 57. K. shakes a nut tree and immediately afterwards picks up the nuts. Shaking and picking up belong together for him, or rather he shakes the tree only in order to be able to pick up nuts. Consequently he would like to have represented both actions in a single figure. This was not possible, so he had to express his experience by drawing both. (Note the over-emphasis in the figure shaking the tree.) A further typical example is fig. 58. D. undresses, hangs up his clothes and gets into the bath. He does not notice that he has drawn himself twice because he is concerned merely with the act of taking a bath. It is typical of this kind of drawing that the figures always appear in the same surroundings. Much more could be said about the other parts of such drawings but this would interrupt the subject matter of this chapter and had therefore better be omitted. But I would remind the reader of the many other examples which belong to this class of phenomena, e.g., fig. 16, hunting for the lost pencil, in which the hand represents the temporally distinct phases of searching and finding ; fig. 7, A. lifts a stone and carries

F

it further ; or fig. 59, B. sneezes, blows his nose, and puts the handkerchief into his pocket, all in one drawing. In these, too, both hands are used to represent movements taking place at different times.

In conclusion I should like to discuss one more illustration thoroughly, although not everything I shall say will belong, strictly speaking, to this chapter. But I feel that from time to time we must direct our attention to wider implications. A particular phenomenon when seen as part of a wider whole will change in significance. It becomes a link in the chain of our phenomenological discussions and it is important to show how the problem of representing temporally different actions appears when considered as one of the many other aspects which we must study. In fig. 60, D. took as his subject " Saying Goodbye ". He is saying goodbye to his father at the end of the holidays before returning to the institution for the blind in Vienna. He is concerned therefore with a profound experience. He begins by drawing the carriage in outline, to indicate its limits. To characterise it he adds the axles with their wheels. Four wheels, of course, because that corresponds to his knowledge. Now he has before him the impression : carriage. Leonardo da Vinci said that every picture should somehow look complete in every one of its phases. He meant, I imagine, that every phase of the picture should leave behind it an impression of completeness so as to enable the spectator to re-live the experiences underlying the creative process. In a sense other than that intended by Leonardo da Vinci this is particularly true of the education of children. By studying the genesis of a picture we have the possibility of investigating the organic interrelationship of the things represented and in this way of experiencing for ourselves the way in which thought processes issue in pictorial form. We see then that when D. had a complete impression of the carriage before him, he considered it necessary first of all to put the carriage on to the rails in order to give it the basis which it had in his thoughts. A carriage without rails is, after all, no carriage. Next he divided the carriage into three compartments in order to create the essential centre for his representation. Thus his attention was concentrated more and more on the true focus of his experience. The part that will ultimately take up his whole attention is treated in more and more detail. Whilst the other compartments do not interest him, he draws in the left one bench and luggage rack, then the steps that lead down and those that lead up. These are, of course, identical. But this treatment has become with him a schema the origin of which we have already discussed in connection with fig. 50. If the drawing had been broken off at this stage and we were to consider it as completed, our eyes would already be immediately guided to the focus of the event. Now D. draws himself. He has taken his place, in the preparation of which he has spent enough time. So now we see him sitting there, holding out his hand in greeting. He has put his luggage in order and has drawn it lying in the luggage rack ; his father stands next to him in the compartment. As he stands next to him his base line has to be drawn. He and his father face one another. This we see from the profiles which are turned towards one another and note that the nose has been accentuated in its importance. " Father already wants to go," D. says, and in order to indicate this he draws higher one foot which he has made shorter than the other. Next the father is outside and waves his hand. D. draws this quite clearly and over-emphasises the waving hand in comparison with the hand which has no function. Then his father remains standing on the platform. Consequently, he has to have that important symbol—a base line. Having now completed the expression of his experience, D. notices the ' empty ' compartment next door and quite automatically lengthens the ' luggage rack ' and puts in two windows. From this final touch the experience dies down and we can ourselves feel vividly the affective space which has been portrayed in this picture. We must ask ourselves whether the feet of the figure representing the father have been neglected on purpose while he was supposed to be moving about inside the compartment, whereas while he is standing outside they have been carefully drawn in. D. explains, " My father puts everything in order in the compartment and then he waits down below until the train goes off." In saying this he indicates that he has represented all the most important phases of his experience. So we return to the starting point of our discussion, having seen how space and time fuse with one another and how the tendencies expressed in the drawing of this picture follow laws of their own that have nothing to do with ' naturalistic ' tendencies.

Sounds, which also have a time sequence, are sometimes depicted as well. Fig. 61a represents a street singer ; 61b a man walking and calling to another that he has lost something and 61c shows a man walking and coughing because a steam roller is throwing up dust. In these drawings K. represents singing, calling out, and coughing by means of characteristic lines. In the case of coughing these are accentuated rhythmically. " You see, he coughs in jerks." I mention these illustrations here because I shall return to this mode of treatment later, when discussing these particular formal problems in relation to primitive art.[1]

(g) A COMPARISON OF THE DRAWINGS OF WEAK SIGHTED AND NORMAL SIGHTED CHILDREN

A comparison of the drawings of weak sighted and normal sighted children is prompted by that most important problem in the art of children, how far the experiences of the sense of sight influence their drawings at all. The answer to this problem could only have been found by studying material such as I have before me produced without the help of the sense of sight. I shall be able to start, therefore, from the fact that the presence of a physical defect has, in the case of the weak sighted children's drawings we have so far studied, prevented visual experience from having more than a quite subsidiary importance. A comparative study should therefore enable us to see clearly what the effect of vision is. Although modern psychologists

---

[1] I have several times in my modelling classes for the blind observed this particular mode of giving shape. " The heart beating with excitement " has been modelled in rhythmical curves, or " blinking " by means of wavy eyelids, or " trembling of the mouth " by means of wavy lips. Cf. *Plastische Arbeiten Blinder*, by Ludwig Münz and Viktor Lowenfeld, plates 23 and 76.

have realised that the art of children is not an expression of visual experiences, there have not hitherto been available suitable examples by means of which one could clearly distinguish the visual from the non-visual sphere. On the other hand it must be remembered that our discussions are of necessity one sided and that consequently many things have had to be omitted which under normal conditions one would expect to see treated in a psychological discussion of the creative art of children. What is lacking above all is a psychological analysis of the correspondence between the development of pictorial art and the total development of the child. But though this is not touched upon we shall gain by having a clearer grasp of the important problems investigated in this book.

In order to be able to compare the drawings of weak sighted with those of normal children, I set a number of subjects of each of which I obtained about one hundred drawings by children of different ages. In this way I obtained approximately two thousand drawings. The first group of subjects was " a street ", " my bedroom," and " a family round a table " and served mainly to compare the treatment of the problem of space. The aim of the second group, " a heavy stone is to be lifted " and " somebody loses a coin and hunts for it, first in a street and then in the dark archway of a house ", was to inquire into the part played by bodily sensations in the creative work of normal children. The third group, " I am shown my presents," was designed to show whether there was emotionally determined over-emphasis. In the following section a special experiment is discussed and the conclusions to be drawn from individual cases are confirmed and extended by a statistical analysis of the whole material.

In studying the first developmental stages of normal children I used, besides the numerous books that deal with this subject, the drawings of my son. These are particularly valuable because I have carefully preserved all his drawings from his first attempt.

In chapter III we considered the scribbling stage and I shall therefore begin now at the point at which the conscious determination of definite forms begins. Even in the case of children of normal sight the order that is assigned to these conceptually perceived forms is not a visual one. So long as the child has no desire for correlation, its drawing is loose and fragmentary. The characteristic things are noted down but they remain without spatial connection and without order. This stage we also find in the weak sighted child where it is even more pronounced. Here, too, it is clear, however, that the order is one of knowledge ; and in ' knowledge ' I include all sensory experiences that promote or mediate this knowledge. The forms that are achieved are therefore a synthesis of many different sensory experiences including, naturally, the experiences of the sense of sight whenever it plays a dominant part in determining the drawing. We can well understand that the child with normal sight frequently emerges earlier out of this stage of setting things down next to each other in a fragmentary way and proceeds to a logically ' ordered ' drawing. We shall see later that in the case of the weak sighted child other senses take a more prominent part. But even in the drawings of my son I was able to observe that the first form relationships were not made on the basis of a visual impression. At the age of $4\frac{1}{2}$ years, after a visit to the zoo, he drew an elephant eating sugar (fig. 62). While his earlier drawings were complete unco-ordinated, we find here that he has made a connection between those parts of the body having functional importance by drawing the path which the sugar takes after it has been swallowed. The legs on the other hand he drew simply next to one another without any connection.

The sense of touch is the one that most corresponds to the sense of sight. But when a weak sighted or blind child is drawing a shape it no more uses its sense of touch than the child with full vision thinks of inspecting visually the object which it is drawing. Both senses are thus ignored ; but naturally this does not imply that the forms produced will be the same since we must assume that touch or sight associations play some part in the creative process. But in both cases a study of the development of the schematic representation of the human figure shows that it is bound to a 'symbol'. I have been able to show that in both cases the schematic line has the same origin and is bound to neither visual nor touch impressions.[1] In chapter III (d) we saw that in the human schema the representative symbols for the different parts of the body are frequently the same as we find illustrated in different works about the art of children. We may therefore assume that neither *the development nor the formal aspects of the human schema have anything whatever to do with the experiences of the sense of sight.* The relation of the individual representative symbols to one another in the case of the weak sighted child is determined by bodily sensations more strongly than in the case of the normal child.

There are greater differences in the treatment of the spatial schema but these are not such as we might have expected because of differences in the mode of space perception. *A priori* one would be inclined to assume that visual and tactual space are in opposition to one another. For we are readily inclined to believe that in the case of a person with full vision, space perception is primarily determined by visual experience and by tactile experience in one who is weak sighted or blind. We might then argue that the minimal visual impressions of the weak sighted correspond to the impressions derived from other senses by the normal sighted. We find, however, that the weak sighted child has to a large extent exactly the same conception of space. The differences are of degree and not of kind. What, we may ask, is the reason? Two possible answers logically suggest themselves. Either normal sighted children do not experience space visually but tactually, like the others ; or, as the visual experiences are not comparable in the two types, both experience space neither visually nor tactually, but *kinaesthetically.*

---

[1] W. Voss maintains that the blind always represent the body as a line. My observations in no way confirm this and I suggest that Voss reached this conclusion only because his pupils lacked adequate technical facilities for expressing themselves. We have seen in previous chapters that the weak sighted child, like the normal child, uses a great variety of symbols.

We shall attempt to throw light on this problem by comparing the drawings of the subjects " Street ", " My Bedroom," and " Family round a Table ", and also by examining a large number of other drawings. It must be emphasised once again, however, that we are concerned only with a comparison of the drawings of *children*, i.e. of drawings which have not progressed beyond the schematic level. The greater part of what follows will be concerned with the problem of how ability develops beyond the schema into a specifically individual, conscious representation of human beings and of space and everything that fills it.

The subjects were chosen for the following reasons. " The Street " was to show the different conceptions of a space that is unlimited yet has a definite direction. " My Bedroom " was to illustrate a closed space and to determine to what extent subjective experience exerts an influence on the normal child and its drawings. When the subject was set, therefore, it was specially emphasised that each child was to draw *his* bedroom and how he lay in his own bed. Finally, " A Family round a Table " was designed to reveal the different conceptions of spatial co-ordination around a centre. I shall in addition refer from time to time to a number of other drawings which, however, have not been collected systematically over various age groups.

The subject " Street " showed that with both normal and weak sighted children the first conscious drawing was a single line. L. Potpeschnigg also found that this was the first stage of development. In the case of both the groups I found that the conception of a base line was predominant. Weak sighted children almost invariably ' folded over ' trees and houses at the sides of the street, while 60 per cent of the normal children did this at the age of seven, 46 per cent at the age of eight, and only 15 per cent at the age of nine. Folding over is still the rule with weak sighted children as late as the eleventh and twelfth year. It is not possible to say whether this difference in development is the result of the different sensory equipment or the steadily increasing influence of school, strongly directed as it is to visual impressions. In any case it is of no importance for our present investigation. Of far greater importance is the realisation that *the same type of formal expression is used by both weak sighted and normal sighted children.* Our next problem will be to investigate up to what point of time a parallel development in the representation of space can be traced. In addition to ' objective space ' we shall examine ' subjective space ', as we have already seen that in both types of children the same impulses are at work.

One group of children was asked to draw a bedroom, any bedroom, whilst other groups were told to draw *their own* bedroom and " you yourself lying in bed ". It was obvious that in " any bedroom " the bed as well as the furniture was drawn in the usual ' orthoscopic ' manner, partly on a base line, partly distributed over the page in any order. (Fig. 63.) " *My* bedroom," on the other hand, as a rule over-emphasised the bed either by exaggerating its size or by drawing it at an angle. Occasionally the surface of the bed was drawn. The immediate surroundings of the bed, too, were drawn with greater care—the things standing on the bedside table, the doll's perambulator under the bed, the clothes on the chair, and so on. The fact that the immediate neighbourhood was thus emphasised indicates that we are dealing with a more intensive space experience. It is not as pronounced as with the weak sighted, but nevertheless it is clearly present. The limits of the bedroom were either not noticed at all or simply shown as a boundary line running around the edges of the paper. One child had drawn the furniture standing on the lower edge of the paper, which served as base line, and I asked him where the corners of the room were. He promptly pointed to the ' corners ' of the paper. I shall therefore have to modify my previous remarks by admitting that the limits of the room as a whole are not unnoticed, although they are not expressly laid down.

Normal children drew " Family round the Table " in as many different ways as the weak sighted. When the food was to be indicated as particularly important, the child chose to draw the table in plan. Chairs drawn in elevation were found as frequently as chairs ' folded over ' to the four sides ; and mixed forms were found whenever it was evident that a special meaning was intended. But if the child wished to describe the table loaded with food and the arrangement of plates, glasses, knives and forks, as well as the form of a jar, he necessarily had to draw the table in plan and the jar in elevation. It is therefore always possible to deduce the intention from the way in which the drawing was made.

It may be of interest in connection with these experiments to give a brief critical survey of the earlier work of others. Georg Kerschensteiner, discussing the " pictorial representation of space " [1] puts first and foremost what he calls " the stage of spacelessness " in which he also includes " linear arrangement " provided it has not been made consciously and systematically. Discussing the latter he speaks of " linear representation proper, which develops quite independently of the other stages ". He shows that the drawing is closely bound up with the line, which may be straight or curved, and " along which the picture develops ". But whenever vertical objects have been folded over in various directions into the plane of the paper, he goes on to speak of " a representation of space which has failed ". Pl. 102 in his book shows a drawing in which space has been treated in exactly the same way as it is usually treated by weak sighted children. To left and right of the street the trees have been folded over. It is plain that he speaks of " spatial representation which has failed " because his criterion is that of naturalistic reproduction. Thus he fails to realise that this way of treating space has its own inherent logical principles that are as valid for this mode of representing space as is perspective, which, after all, also obeys only certain laws.

Levinstein speaks of a " spatial ideal schema ",[2] in which all objects standing on the ground have a common line as their support. He, too, fails to recognise the laws according to which this support or basis is treated. But

[1] *Die Entwicklung der zeichnerischen Begabung*, Munich.
[2] *Untersuchungen über das Zeichnen des Kindes bis zum 14. Lebensjahr.*

they are as clear in the illustrations he gives as they are in the work of weak sighted children. In his illustrations of *Hans guck' in die Luft* (Johnny nose-in-the-air) we find cases of folding up and folding over that clearly show the connection with the base line. We find, too, excellent examples of what I have called " affective space ", which Levinstein did not notice and does not discuss. He merely speaks of " confusing plan and elevation " without showing that behind this apparent confusion lies a definite intention.

In the work collected by Oscar Wulff [1] we detect the same tendencies as in the drawings of weak sighted children. He speaks of " the schema of linear arrangement. . . ." " But then the sensations of standing on the ground make themselves felt and in the base line create for themselves an abstract means of expression. . . ." " Not only houses and trees but also irregularities in the landscape are placed on the base line, or this may begin to rise and fall so that profiles result." (See figs. 41–49.) He also speaks of ' folding over ' as creating spatial appearances. " The further development of the spatial schema necessarily leads to a confusion of various forms and means of expression. Plan and elevation no longer as before alternate in different parts but begin to be inextricably intermingled in the sense of a birds eye view. . . ." " Thus it may happen that a lake or a pond is placed in birdseye view above the base line. Similarly, individual figures and rows of trees with their base lines or the strip of ground seen from above are simply drawn upwards at an angle. Consequently at this early stage the figures may be at right angles to the strip so that they lie at an angle in the picture or even upside down." (See fig. 53.) Thus Wulff merely describes the way in which ' objective space ' is represented without in any way discussing the inner relationships of this method of treating space. Nevertheless we see how complete is the correspondence between these drawings and those of weak sighted children.

[1] *Die Kunst des Kindes.*

In conclusion we may refer to the work of Gustav Britsch,[1] who also discusses the problems of how space is represented in drawing.   Britsch discusses clearly and convincingly the laws underlying the pictorial relationships of objects in space.   His abstract and philosophical treatment of the formal principles of composition shows " that the drawings of the child are symbols of a specific mental unity, of a definite stage in the interrelationship of concepts.   Those very things that seem strange or false to the adult express the fact that at his own level the child has a unified conception and clearly expresses his meaning ".

From this Britsch correctly concludes that it is inadmissible when speaking of " trees folded over ", to attempt to connect the specific concepts of the child with those of the adult.   Such a view is the only correct one ;   and if we recognise that the drawings of children follow laws of their own we shall no longer apply judgments of right and wrong to them in the same way as we do to the drawings of adults.

We may sum up by saying that the comparative study of the way in which space is depicted by weak sighted and normal children has shown that in both cases we are dealing with phenomena that, independently of visual experience, follow laws of their own.   That these laws of infantile thinking are consistent and common to all children we were able to show in particular by studying the properties of the base line, which we found in all cases to be determined by somatic experience.   Affective space derives its characteristics from subjective sense impressions of a special kind and, with especial clarity, illustrates the relationship of the person to that which he is depicting.

Let us now turn to the second group of topics and examine the part played in children's drawing by somatic feelings and expressive overemphasis.

When the subject " a heavy stone is to be lifted " was set, each child was urged to try for himself how difficult it was to lift a large stone.   He was then to draw his own experience.   In the earliest drawings it is almost the rule that the arms are overemphasised and the representative

---

[1] *Theorie der bildenden Kunst*, Munich, 1926.

symbols for hands especially accentuated. Up to the ninth year such drawings occur very frequently. But gradually, as the children become more and more able to perceive forms and movement, the majority passes beyond this stage. By the age of 13 only isolated cases remain to show that somatic feelings preceded other sensory impressions. In the drawings of the weak sighted, somatic experience still remains the generating principle, but plays only a subsidiary role in the works of normal children. We have also to remember that in the earliest children's drawings overemphasis of the arms may result from the fact that the child knows of no other way to depict movement.

The experiment with " the lost coin " provides clearer and still more convincing evidence. The task was set as follows : " You are visiting your uncle. He gives you a coin. On your way home you lose the coin on the street. At last you find it. Now you come to the porch of your house. You go in. In the passage it is dark. As luck will have it you again lose the coin. You hunt for it in the dark. Now draw the search, first in the street and then in the dark house." A large number of children drew themselves far larger in the dark house than on the well lighted street. We may conclude from this that there is a greater awareness of the body in the dark (cf. fig. 64). When one is alone and concentrating on the lost coin the intensity of self-consciousness is greater and this finds its impression in the overemphasised drawing. This indicates that the weak sighted do not need to be taught to use this sort of experience as a guiding principle for their drawings. In fact we may conclude that they are bound to a far higher degree than the normal sighted to their bodily experiences.

When external objects are emphasised the matter is somewhat different. The topic, " You for the first time see your presents on the table," was set shortly before the children were in fact to be given presents so that adequate tension was created. There can be no doubt that the presents became the most important element in the drawing regardless of other things which necessarily or in addition were included in it. 'Right' or 'wrong' as judgments applied to the proportions become inapplicable when the picture has an emphatic psychological meaning. How grandly we see the consciousness of coming possession, the surprise, displayed in the drawing ! (Fig. 65.) Here the magnitude of the experience finds a perfect expression. We could continue indefinitely to illustrate these facts showing to what a high degree infantile drawings are determined by value judgments (fig. 66).

It is clear now that here, too, it is not justifiable to speak of 'misproportions' or 'false relationships of size'. It is impossible to share the views of Levinstein who maintains that "children have no conception of proportion. Different parts are drawn too large or too small ". They are not simply " drawn too large or too small ". Their sizes are intended to express the significance of the child's experiences. One can also accept only with the greatest reservation Kerschensteiner's statement about children's earliest drawings, " at this stage the forms of the body, the places where the limbs are attached, the relative sizes of parts of the body and so on, are of no concern to the child." Let us rather bear in mind what Hartlaub [1] says : " A child at play does not merely want to tell or place before himself what he knows, but rather those parts of his knowledge that seem to him *important*." (And, we may add, that which at the moment of creation has impulsive force.) " That important things are remembered is in the main determined by feeling though we do not mean this in a subjectivistic sense. This explains on the one hand that so essential characteristic of children's sketches, the involuntary omission of all unimportant things, and on the other the choice of size as a measure of the degree of importance." In looking at children's drawings we must therefore regard it as a fundamental desideratum that general æsthetic or naturalistic comparisons must be excluded. The formative principles have to be sought in specific impulses and we have shown that these impulses follow laws of their own that lie outside the naturalistic

[1] G. F. Hartlaub, *Der Genius im Kinde*, Breslau, 1922.

laws of form. It is of vital importance that the teacher should study the origins of those characteristics frequently still regarded as ' mistakes ' or ' misproportions '. He will find that his efforts are richly rewarded and that he will obtain insight into some of the obscure corners of the child's mind.

From a comparison of the bodily experiences and the overemphases found in the drawings of weak sighted and normal children respectively we must conclude that expressive overemphases are formative factors to the same degree in both cases. We have though to decide for each individual whether the forms have been determined by visual or by haptic experience, or whether they spring from conceptual thinking, joy or pain. Further, our investigations have clearly shown that in the pictorial art of the weak sighted, bodily experience is an integrating factor among the various instinctive creative components, whilst in the drawings of children with normal vision it plays a more subordinate part in the totality of their creative work.

If we include in these comparisons the facts already noted about the corresponding treatment accorded by normal as well as weak sighted children to the problems of time and space, it is clear that the work of both groups has the same creative basis and the same formal characteristics. From this it follows that a large part of the work of normal sighted children is not determined by visual experiences. We must conclude, therefore, that because weak sighted children are more intensely bound up with experiences of the self and above all because they lack visual impressions, *it is in their drawings that the essential formal characteristics of the art of all children as such are to be seen in their purest form.* This in turn leads to the conclusion that almost all my investigations, which up to this point have been concerned exclusively with the work of weak sighted children, are also applicable to the work of normal children. Thus our discussions have led us far beyond the framework of a merely specialist investigation and have achieved universal validity.

(*h*) THE DEVELOPMENT OF THE DRAWING OF NORMAL CHILDREN,
STUDIED BY MEANS OF ONE TOPIC SET WITH SPECIAL REFERENCE
TO CERTAIN PROBLEMS OF FORM

In order to study the importance of haptic and also other problems of form at different developmental stages, the same topic was given to a number of children whose ages varied from six to fifteen. When choosing the topic I tried to take into account the developmental possibilities of visual as well as of haptic and emotional expressive experiences. The topic was, " you are under an apple tree. On one of its lower branches you see an apple which you particularly admire and which you would like to have. You stretch out your hand to pick the apple, but your reach is just about a span too short. Then you make a great effort and get the apple after all. Now you have it and enjoy eating it. Draw yourself as you are taking the apple off the tree." The results showed that without being influenced in any way the children were freely able to display the pattern of their experiences. ' Beautiful ' trees and apples were drawn just as often as ' misproportioned ' people. The subject had allowed the child to be absorbed in the visual experiences of the *beautiful* apple hanging on one of the lower branches of the tree, as much as into the feeling of the *importance* attained by the apple when it is particularly desired. The haptic experience of *grasping* the apple could be expressed just as much as the experience of *stretching* the body while it was being picked. At each age group I obtained 40–50 drawings, a total of some 400, and these form the material for the following discussion. I considered separately the representation of the individual human being, the representation of the tree, and the relation of the two to one another. These relations are analysed in the appended tables.

At the fifth and six year the great majority of children drew a merely schematic tree. They did not, for instance, especially emphasise the importance of the apple. But in most cases the stretching of the body or the arm was expressed by strong overemphasis (fig. 67). We see that at this early age visual impressions play almost no part in the drawing whilst the experience of the body, on the other hand, strongly influences the various forms. The graphs of Table 5 show that the inflexible schema of man and tree are in opposite phases of their development. In this connection as before, I use the term inflexible schema when it is impossible to deduce a particular representational intention from the form of the drawing. Only about 1 per cent of the children drew an inflexible human schema at the age of five. At the age of six 16·3 per cent drew an inflexible schema whilst 83·7 per cent of the drawings at this age showed overemphases. If we take into consideration the high percentage of merely schematic trees the representation of which is not determined by any special intention, we may conclude that this early infantile mode of representation is to a high degree bound up with subjective experiences.

We see that until the tenth year there is a steady increase up to almost 50 per cent of children who draw inflexible human schemata. At the same time overemphases in depicting 'myself' gradually decrease. We next discover that the proportion of inflexible tree schemata and of emphasis of the apple or the branch on which it hangs decrease and we may conclude that at about this time more and more attention is paid to the environment whilst the importance of the self for the drawing decreases. Nevertheless we should note that at this stage of development the overemphasis of the branch or the apple is determined by feeling rather than by vision. This is clear from the fact that most of the branches have not been thought and depicted as continuations of the tree but frequently appear separated from it and drawn in the middle of the paper thus expressing the importance of the apple and the branch for the child. If we regard the isolated branch and the overemphasis of the apple as expressions of value judgments about the environment, we see that at the age of nine 69·5 per cent and at the age of ten 64·8 per cent of the children still draw according to principles of valuation. This representation of the environment in terms of personal judgments of value has its peak at the tenth and eleventh year and implies that the degree to which the child is bound up with its bodily experience diminishes. Consequently, on the one hand the inflexible human schema begins to appear, and on the other, increasing conceptual knowledge of the external world and its significance lowers the child's capacity for coordinating visual and other impressions in the drawing. This is borne out by the figures, for in the ninth and tenth years 44 and 43 per cent respectively of the children were unable to establish a relationship between child and tree. *This period, then, represents the time at which the confidence of the child in its own creative power is for the first time shaken by the fact that it is becoming conscious of the significance of its environment.* The teacher clearly feels this period as being one of crisis. At this time children get into difficulties over their methods of representing space. Some of them perceive that ' folding over ' is a " mistake ". The conditions of thinking, which previously had been so deeply rooted in the child, are disturbed. The ' fundamental laws ' begin to waver. The well known mixed forms now appear in which plan and elevation collide and no longer, as at earlier ages, result from a definite intention. At this time the child rather uncertainly lets trees standing on both sides of the street grow ' upwards ' whereas previously they had in most cases been related to the base line. As the perception of form and size matures, however, the capacity for coordination again increases. We see from the graph that the conscious perception of individual forms begins as the capacity for relating various objects develops.

One of the essentials of realistic representation is the ability to assign certain characteristic features correctly within the total form. Up to the ninth year the proportions as well as the method of treatment clearly show that the human figure is emphasised relatively to the tree ; but in the twelfth year the proportion of figural overemphasis sinks to 13 per cent whilst the overemphasis of the tree reaches its peak, 47 per cent. This is a clear measure of the intensity of visual experience, which at this time begins to have a powerful effect. The graph showing the development of realistic representation shows that after the end of the fourteenth year this remains stationary. 66 per cent achieve realistic representation of the human being at least in intention, whilst this is the case for 97 per cent of the drawings of trees.[1] About half the children included in the 97 per cent had chosen to depict merely part of the tree (see Table 3b). They drew only a branch with one apple. But it is quite clear that the branch is in most cases thought of as part of a tree, that is, it has a visual or tactile basis and is not a conceptual symbol (compare with this the high percentage of branches appearing in the ninth year). In the eleventh year 45 per cent of the children preferred to draw a branch but by the thirteenth year this proportion has sunk to 19·5 per cent. During this time, in which the importance of visual experience first becomes an integral part of the experience of form, it is the magnitude of the appearance of the tree that enters the world of experience of the child and dominates its creative powers. Only gradually does the child begin to have an eye for detail. We must therefore interpret the 50 per cent who in the fifteenth year isolate the branch from the total conception of ' tree ' as having succeeded in differentiating between their sensory experiences.

The fundamentally important question now arises as to the position of that 33 per cent which was unable to achieve a realistic representation of the human figure. It consisted of those whose creative type did not allow them to co-ordinate the separate parts ' correctly '. Among them we find ' misproportions ', or apparently schematic representations, which up to the present have been regarded as the work of untalented children and dismissed as such. From the point of view of the psychology of form it is quite irrelevant to regard the drawings as ' good ' or ' bad ', that is, to make value judgments about them. I shall therefore exclude qualitative considerations altogether and attend to the

---

[1] This merely represents the proportion of ' realistic intentions ' and does not mean that 97 per cent of the children were actually able to draw with realistic accuracy.

' mistakes ', the investigation of which promises to be more fruitful than merely giving them an æsthetic label.

We usually speak of faulty drawings when some aspect or other does not correspond to our visual perception. Even the psychologist speaks of ' faulty representations ' whenever he has failed to study the sources of error. Let us take the opposite path and assume hypothetically that no error is a result of a lapse of knowledge but springs from a representational *intention*. By analysing the drawings of weak sighted children I have shown that the investigation of such ' mistakes ' often allows us to penetrate deeply into the roots of experience. Now it is extremely interesting to observe that we are able to deduce a representational intention even in the case of the ' mistakes of form ' in the drawings of those children taking part in this experiment who did not achieve a realistic representation.

Figs. 77 *a* and *b* show that the overemphases and misproportions, the omission of some forms and the addition of others not apparently present, spring from the *personal* experience of shapes and movements, the stimulus for which is not visual. For the present I shall leave the matter at this general observation, as this test series was not designed to show more than the development and significance of, or rather the differentiation between, visual and nonvisual formative principles. A thorough psychological discussion of the two creative types will be undertaken in the second part of this volume.

(i) THE TYPES OF ARTISTIC TALENT

Many teachers have found from their practical experience that the ability to draw manifests itself quite differently in two types ; but up to the present the psychological basis of these differences has not been discovered. Kerschensteiner, in his many sided book, *Die Entwicklung der Zeichnerischen Begabung*, speaks of four stages in the representation of space. The last he calls " the stage of correct pictorial representation ", which shows that he is exclusively concerned with the visual perception of space, whose zenith is reached in the realistic drawing of perspective. " Next

TABLE 3A

(Figures are percentages)

Representation of the Human Figure

Age in Years	6	7	8	9	10	11	12	13	14
Inflexible Schema	16·3	29·6	35·7	48·5	31·2	25·5	13·9	9	0
Overemphasis of the arm	65·1	51·8	50·0	30·3	37·5	32·7	33·3	27·5	21·2
Overemphasis of body length	18·6	18·6	14·3	21·2	15·6	7·0	2·8	3·0	12·2
Realistic Representation	0	0	0	0	16·7	34·8	50·0	60·5	66·6

TABLE 3B

Representation of the Tree

Age in Years	6	7	8	9	10	11	12	13	14
Inflexible Schema	81·6	57·1	43·3	30·5	29·8	23·2	8·3	3·0	0
Branch and Apple alone	15·6	35·7	36·7	47·3	45·1	39·5	19·5	39·3	50
Overemphasis of Apple	2·8	7·2	20·0	22·2	19·7	2·3	13·8	6·1	3·0
Realistic Representation	0	0	0	0	6·4	62·8	80·5	78·8	97·0

TABLE 4

(Figures are in percentages)

Relation of Tree and Human Figure in the Drawing

Age in Years	6	7	8	9	10	11	12	13	14	15
No Relation	26	28·2	37·1	44·5	43·4	19·2	11·6	2·7	3	0
Overemphasis of Figure		61·5	59·2	40·7	42·4	41·9	25·2	13·1	39·4	28·1
Overemphasis of Tree		7·7	3·7	14·8	15·2	26	30·3	47·1	21·2	9·4
Realistic Representation		2·6*	0	0	0	12·9	32·5	36·1	36·4	62

* This includes a case of special talent

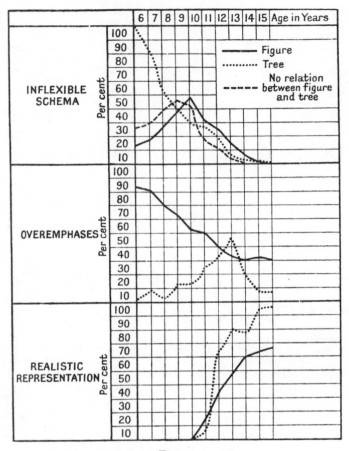

TABLE 5

Topic : " You are under an apple tree. On it you see a particularly fine apple, which you would like to have. It is hanging on one of the lower branches. You stretch out your hand to pick it but cannot reach it by about a span. However, you make a great effort and at last get it after all. Draw yourself getting the apple off the tree ! "

to these four stages," says Kerschensteiner, " there is another, linear representation proper, which, quite independently of the others, develops to the highest artistic expression.[1] I have no doubt that these linear representations proper are in no way intended either by the child or in the art of primitive peoples to give a pictorial representation of space." What Kerschensteiner here means by " a pictorial representation of space " is obviously that one which springs from the experience of visual perception. He drew this conclusion from the enormous amount of material at his disposal and I regard it as an important indication of a fact that also emerges from my own experience. L. Potpeschnigg[2] quite misconstrues the essential consistency of the child's representation of spatial forms and therefore speaks of ' mistakes ' in the representation of space. Nevertheless her own investigations lead her to conclude that these ' mistakes ' of spatial representation may persist for a very long time in the development of the child. She points out that " in the less talented these mistakes are never transcended " and thus proves from her own experience that there is one type which retains this particular mode of drawing spatial forms. Richard Rothe,[3] Inspector of Drawing for Vienna, says that his wide experience has led him to distinguish two types that differ in their mode of creation. The first type builds up its drawings out of separate parts " as one would build with bricks and stones ". He calls this the ' building type ' in contrast to the ' seeing type '. " The seeing type proceeds quite differently. He moulds the form he is aiming at out of a single piece. He holds in his hand the piece of clay with which he is working and turns it round and round whilst at work. . . . While he is working he thinks of a definite figure in a definite posture. In his memory a specific *visual experience* is active. . . . If we compare these totally different modes of creating forms and the differences of technique, we have to conclude that there are two desires, two directions, two aims, which we cannot force into the same mould." Bühler describes

---

[1] Kerschensteiner is referring to pictures in which the base line is of predominating importance and in which the solution of the problems of space takes the form of characteristic ' strips '.

[2] L. Potpeschnigg, *Aus der Kindheit der Bildenden Kunst*, Leipzig, 1912.

[3] Cf. *Die Quelle, Vereinigte Monatschefte für Pädagogische Reform*, and *Kunst und Schule*, 1930, No. 12.

the one as the synthetic and the other as the analytic procedure. G. F. Hartlaub goes too far when he says " the more strongly ' visions ' predominate in the work of a a child, the more unusual is the artistic talent of that particular child. As we have seen every child, not only the untalented, can draw ideographically. It is only genius that shows itself in visual forms and in addition to the powers of memory, also arouses the necessary technical abilities ".[1] Hartlaub thus denies that ' ideographic representation ' is capable of development and regards visual experience as exclusively artistic although he admits that there are non-visual ' talents '.

It is clear then that all mentioned writers agree that the development of realistic representation occurs only in a certain number of pupils, those for whom *visual experience* provides the starting point for their work. The origin of the artistic experience of the other creative type must now be subjected to a more detailed analysis.

[1] *Der Genius im Kinde.*

CHAPTER IV

VISUAL PERCEPTION AND HAPTIC PERCEPTION

(a) THE CONCEPTS OF VISUAL AND HAPTIC PERCEPTION

To be able to separate pure optical perception from other sense impressions we need an object of contemplation that cannot be influenced or disturbed by other senses. But associatively almost everything in our surroundings somehow influences our sensations and experiences. We can therefore hardly speak of *pure* optical perception of things. Even colour, regarded in isolation from any object, awakes in us dark, bright, cheerful, or warm feelings, and it seems self-evident that, for example, a tree waving in the wind awakes in us some knowledge of the elasticity of the wood, the nature of the leaves, and so on. Thus Van Gogh writes in a letter to his brother, " Yesterday evening I concerned myself with the gently rising terrain of the wood, which is completely covered with dry, dead beech leaves. . . . The problem is—and I find this extremely difficult—to bring out the depth of the colour and the enormous strength and firmness of the soil. . . . Out of this soil grow the trunks of the beeches, which are a shining green on the side on which they are brightly illuminated, whilst on the shadow side the trunks show a warm, strong black-green. . . . I am affected and intrigued to see how strongly the trunks are rooted in the ground. I began to paint them with the brush, and was unable to bring out the characteristics of the soil, which had already been painted in thick colours. The new brush strokes simply disappeared. Therefore I pressed roots and trunks out of the tube and modelled them a little with my brush. There, now they stand in it, grow out of it, and have firmly taken root." [1]

We see here how the optical impression has been influenced

[1] Vincent van Gogh, *Letters.*

and formed by other sense impressions. Can optical perception therefore be adequately conceived by means of seeing with the eye alone ? We shall have to conclude that optical perception in its purest form is only an extreme case of visual perception in general. We must therefore use the term ' visual perception ' when impressions coming from other senses are subordinate to those coming from the eye, and when visual impressions are the dominant feature in a percept.

The artistic representation of visual impressions always starts from optical perception. It is concerned with the subjective experience of the self only in so far as any creative activity is an individual mental act. " Being bound to the self " in this sense is not what we shall understand by the term later, because it does not seek its experience in bodily sensations but outside the body. The self merely applies judgments of value to the experience.

The further optical experience recedes into the background the less important does the eye become as the intermediary of the concept. To the same extent the importance of the environment diminishes and experience is more and more confined to the processes that go on in the body as a whole, bodily sensations, muscular innervations, deep sensibilities, and their various emotional effects. As the importance of the sense of sight diminishes so that of the sense of touch as the intermediary between sensations and the concept increases. In what follows we shall mean by ' haptic perception ' the synthesis between tactile perceptions of external reality and those subjective experiences that seem to be so closely bound up with the experience of self.

(b) HAPTIC PERCEPTION AS A BASIS FOR CREATIVE WORK

Inferior visual awareness is not always necessarily determined by a physical defect of the eyes. In the previous chapter we distinguished clearly between physical and psychological sight. Haptic perception must therefore be considered as a separate type and we shall have to investigate how far creative work can be determined by it. We shall start with some observations made by me in the course of my long experience as a teacher.

(1) A pupil of the Institute for the Blind who still had considerable visual acuity modelled as though he were completely blind, without in the slightest degree using his visual powers. His products had all the typical characteristics of the plastic art of the blind (Plate 78 *a* and *b*). He began his modelling with easily recognizable individual symbols, and proceeded from them to develop a steadily more unified form. At this time he was given eye exercises for the weak sighted and so began to be aware of the possibilities of sight. His plastic work gradually lost its expressiveness. He began to repeat certain types of expression which showed that the last form he developed (Plate 78*b*) did not represent the true nature of his creative impulses.[1] All the models he made after this one contained, like his earlier ones, clearly distinguishable and frequently isolated representations of form and expression ; but the forms and their expressiveness remained stationary (cf. Plate 67*b*). The more he used his eyes the less pleasure he took in his work and he finally gave it up altogether.

(2) Another case, one among many, shows the same result but in the reverse order. G. S. (cf. Table 1), when he began to draw for the first time, tried to the utmost of his ability to use his rudimentary powers of sight although he hardly used them at all when modelling. He clearly believed that drawing as contrasted with modelling was concerned with the use of the eyes and that therefore he had to re-orientate himself. All his products, however, were uniform, undifferentiated, and without expressiveness (Plate 57*a*). Only when he ' freed ' himself of his visual impressions did his drawings begin to achieve the expressiveness of a personal experience (Plates 28, 31 *a* and *b*).

Both these cases showed that ' haptic perception ' was intimately concerned with the development of artistic power. In other words it became the basis of creative

---

[1] Plate 78*b* shows the last in a series of modellings developed under the direction of L. Münz and discussed by him in his book, *Plastische Arbeiten Blinder*.

activity. If we ask ourselves why the first case ceased to work and the second began to achieve and to delight in real work we may perhaps contribute something to an understanding of this phenomenon.

Both cases, as their work showed, were non-visual types and used their eyes only under external compulsion. So long as no foreign influences were at work the first case could create freely. But as soon as the introduction of a course in normal writing and reading drew his attention to the possibilities of sight, his conceptualisation lost its power and unity. The disharmony between his basic type and the training he received destroyed his belief in his creative powers. He gave up working altogether because his visual powers were insufficient—he was able to use them only with great effort and difficulty—and because visual experiences were not the sources of his creative impulses.

The second case leads to similar conclusions. Because of practical educational considerations, G.S. had from the beginning been urged to use to their fullest extent what visual powers he had ; but this only threw him into a state of conflict. When he was induced to draw, he believed that the visual abilities he had acquired necessarily had to be used in drawing. But here again the ability to see was a product of training and was not essential to the true nature of his creative activity. It was only when I succeeded in freeing him of this belief, by getting him to draw specially selected themes, that his creative activity was freed of its inhibition. After that the eye served not as the intermediary for his conceptions, but merely to control the technical details while working.

Both cases show clearly how fundamentally important it is for teachers to realise that the nature of creative expression is bound up with haptic perception whenever this is the artist's basic and habitual mode of experience.

(c) HAPTIC PERCEPTION AND THE EXPERIENCE OF THE SELF

In this section I shall be concerned only with the facts of self experience and not with its effects on the problems of form. The latter will be considered in the next chapter.

The world of those who ' see haptically ' is a world confined
to things that can be perceived by means of our senses
of touch or bodily sensations.   In this world the eye does
not mediate between reality and the concept.   Comparative
examples will be found in Plates 1 to 4, which deal with
the same subject and were made under the same external
conditions.   In them we can see clearly the differences
between experiences arising out of visual impressions and
those arising out of more personal feelings.   In Pl. 2 the
experiences are centred in Moses alone and in how in his
anger he struck the rock so that water should come out
of it.   Pl. 1, on the other hand, shows us a ' spectacle '.
How grand it is to *see* that water flows out of the rock !
In Pl. 2 nothing but haptic experiences are embodied.
The experience of form is autoplastic, intensely personal
and finds its strongest expression in the lineaments of Moses.
In Pl. 1 we feel that we are taking part in this great moment
as *spectators*.   In the former everything has been concentrated on expression and gesture ;   in the latter it is the
arrangement of the figures, the rich ornamentation, the
colours, all that is visually perceivable, which has become
the main problem of representation.   Many of the figures
are stylised and their relation to the subject of the picture
can only be seen from the movement of individual groups.
We see that Moses and the elders of the people are raising
their arms as a sign of the great miracle that has just
occurred.   Others have jars with which to fetch water.   A
mother is holding her child so that it may drink, and so on.
Nowhere in this picture, however, do we perceive those
intense personal sensations that hold our attention on Pl. 2
in which even the water, the only thing outside the person
of Moses, has been drawn in a compact mass as though it
could be grasped.   The fact that in this picture the arm has
been ' added ' later also shows clearly the synthetic mode
of procedure characteristic of haptic types.   This will be
discussed in more detail in a later chapter.   I must once
again emphasise that both drawings were made in one
classroom under exactly the same conditions.

A comparison of Pls. 3 and 4 will perhaps bring out

even more clearly the antithesis between visual and haptic perception. In Pl. 3 the landscape and everything in it has become the main problem in the picture, and the dreaming Jacob fits naturally into his environment. But in Pl. 4 an intense personal experience is concentrated in the figure. Jacob is dreaming and in his dreams he feels that something is happening round about him. But only the ' imaginary ' lines drawn away from him lead us to what might be happening outside his person, the landscape with floating angels, which in the other picture has become the central topic. Here again we experience the strength of the concentration on bodily and muscular sensations, which find their formal expression in autoplastic drawing. Haptic perception, then, is to the highest degree bound to the self, intensely subjective. Its formal representations can thus be clearly distinguished from those of visual perception.

Chapter V

THE TWO CREATIVE TYPES

We can clearly distinguish two types both by the end products of their artistic activities and by their attitude to their own experiences. Compared with the blind the weak sighted possess a great degree of visual acuity though it is little enough when compared with full normal sight. Nevertheless their attitudes show clearly whether their world is that of people with sight or that of the blind, in other words, whether theirs is an optic or a haptic world. Hearing is excluded in both cases, as we are dealing with pictures. Some weak sighted people immediately apply their eyes closely to anything which attracts their attention, even if they have only the most rudimentary vision. Others, even though they possess considerable visual power, approach everything through the sense of touch and use their eyes only when some external factor compels them to do so. The former try to maintain contact with their environment also visually. They react strongly to light stimuli and are visually easily distracted. The latter react exclusively to haptic stimuli. Let us call the first the *visual type* ; and the other the *haptic type*, although both designations are imperfect. When we investigate the artistic products of these two types we find that the visual type starts from his environment, that his concepts are developed into a perceptual whole through the fusion of partial visual experiences. The haptic type, on the other hand, is primarily concerned with his own body sensations and with the tactual space around him. Let us first examine the visual type, as it approximates more closely to the ' normal '.

(a) THE VISUAL TYPE

The immediate mental assimilation of the experiences of the sense of sight is usually regarded as the decisive factor in the specific nature of artistic activity. As we are discussing the weak sighted, however, we have to remember that their activities deviate somewhat from the normal because on the whole they are concerned only in the second place with visual impressions and experiences. We may speak of these as secondary optical impressions because physical disabilities on the whole prevent primary optical experiences. And as the world of visual concepts is to some extent inhibited by physical disability,[1] it would be more accurate to use the term ' inhibited visual type '. Nevertheless the psychological orientation of persons of this type is towards visual experience. Consequently they must be regarded as corresponding to what common aesthetics regards as the more normal type. Their visual impressions are achieved mainly synthetically by being built up out of partial impressions. Though they may start with a visual image representing their ideal conception of a picture, the picture itself is arrived at through a constructive synthesis. Through this method of putting together partial impressions that may have been aroused optically, dynamically, or in some other way, though the original conception was a visual one, the superficial effect may well be impressionistic (cf. Pl. 37, " Street Battle " ; Pl. 38, " Speaker "). But the impressionistic appearance is purely superficial and is not fundamental, because the impressionist creates the appearance of a whole by analytic means. The aim of the impressionist is to achieve a dynamic apprehension of the total impression. But in the cases we are discussing the total impression is created purely synthetically because the immediate apprehension of the whole is physically impossible. A more detailed investigation of some pictures of this type will lead to greater clarity.

Pl. 5 represents a drowning man. It is characteristic of this stage of drawing that because visual impressions are lacking, expressive gestures can be represented only by means of symbols. The lines of pathos under the eyes and also those leading from the nose to the mouth show that there has been no deep, conscious experience of form and expression. They are undifferentiated symbols. As this

---

[1] See Löwenfeld, B., " Zur Blindenpsychologie," *Zeitschr. f. d. Oesterr. Blindenwesen*, xii, No. 7–8.

drawing was made during an early stage of development, everything was reduced to the simplest formal symbols. The most striking fact about this ' mask ', however, is the special way in which the eyes have been treated. It is characteristic of this particular creative type that the whole experience should have been concentrated in the eyes. " As the whole eye is full of water I can see nothing but water around me," Sch. G. says (cf. Table I, No. 3). Consequently he paints enormously exaggerated blue eyes that for him mirror the essential experience of the drowning man. It is significant that this experience is concentrated in the organ of sight. Similar exaggerations are found in many masks of primitive peoples and in a special chapter we shall concern ourselves with the parallelism of primitive and expressive art to the phenomena discussed here. In passing we may mention that this particular mode of representation is closely related to the masks of New Mecklenburg in the Bismarck Archipelago. Sch. G's picture was determined by his subjective experience whereas the ancestral mask was designed to have a frightening, demonic effect. Nevertheless both exaggerations have the same psychological origin. Both point to the parts whose expressions are specially significant and both achieve this by the same means. So far, a distinction of creative types has not yet been discussed. Nevertheless it was psychologically interesting to see that the decisive factor for this type was the stimulation of the *organ of sight.*

Let us next consider Pls. 13 *a* and *b* (Forest), Pl. 40 (Fire), Pl. 33 (Accident), and Pl. 37 (Street Battle). These pictures are especially characteristic products of this type. The striking fact about them is that they are all concerned with depicting the things round about us, whilst the pictures of the haptic type are always concerned with depicting the effect of the experience on the person himself. *Through his drawings the visual type wants to bring the outer world closer to himself, whilst the haptic type is above all concerned with projecting his inner world into the picture.* In the pictures of the visual type we shall always find that visual experiences, such as the colour contrast between light and dark, are particularly emphasised (cf. Plates 32 and 33). Pl. 33 (Accident) is a particularly striking example ; we might almost describe it as an ode to light. Because there is a physical disturbance of the sense of sight the integrative efforts of the visual type follow lines of their own ; but it is important to notice that the sense of sight is always the final court of appeal.

(b) THE HAPTIC TYPE

The haptic type approximates, with certain reservations to be discussed later, to the type of the completely blind. The basis of his impressions is always haptic perception. With the exception of colour experiences, which will be discussed in a following chapter, everything springs from his immediate bodily experiences. Just as the blind start from a ' primitive shape ' to which expressive symbols are separately added, so the weak sighted proceed from a ' primitive outline ' to which the symbols for expression are added later.[1] A blind pupil first models the eye balls, then places them into the eye sockets, after which he pulls the lids over them. In a very similar way a weak sighted pupil frequently draws the eye cavity first (cf. Pl. 22). Then he adds the eye and the pupil and finally draws the eyelid over it. In the same way he first draws the mouth cavity with the teeth and later adds the lips in exactly the same way as the blind pupil sets to work. These facts, but particularly the way in which the individual symbols of expression are added to a picture, show clearly how closely the spatial perception of this weak sighted type is related to that of the blind. We can go further and conclude that as these two creative types are so different, the mode of creation has nothing to do with the degree of visual acuity. Extreme cases, which I found to be by no means rare, proved that, according to the mode of their creative activity, some people with full sight must be classified with the non-visual blind and, conversely, that many blind people have to be regarded as visual types.

We shall next discuss some of these extreme cases. This

[1] Cf. L. Münz and V. Lowenfeld, *Plastische Arbeiten Blinder*. Brünn : Rohrer, 1934.

will show conclusively that to consider the organ of sight alone is quite insufficient to give us insight into productive activities and the mental reproduction of our environment. It will also become clear that the concept of weak sightedness has to be redefined without special reference to the organ of sight.

Case 1. The following is an interesting case because it is extreme and pure and occurred while I was teaching normal sighted children to draw. A thirteen year old boy was completely incapable of achieving any kind of picture. All my efforts failed. Under no circumstances could he be brought to conceive of visual percepts. As nothing availed, it occurred to me to try to treat him as I do the blind or the weak sighted. I therefore deflected his attention altogether from visual impressions and asked him to control his images by means of tactual impressions alone. The subjects I set him were all such that they could be translated into bodily experiences. The boy began to work and in his drawings the formal and expressive symbols were exactly those to be found in the work of the weak sighted. In Pl. 6 (a drowning man) the representation is still somewhat more uncertain than in its successor, Pl. 7 (Moses Breaks the Stone Tablets). We notice at first sight the contrast between the completely mechanised representation of the waves, which have been constructed purely conceptually and symbolised by a wavy line, and the subjective, strongly expressive representation of the head. This contrast alone shows how closely the picture is bound up with subjective experiences that are typical of the haptic type and have nothing to do with visual impressions. The setting sun whose circle is sinking into the sea is a beautiful poetic representation ; but the experiences from which it springs are unrelated to the visual field. Let us examine the head more closely. We notice that the lines carrying the expression do not have their basis in anatomical or visual facts. They spring from bodily sensations and are ' lines of force ' resulting from the interaction of different muscular tensions. The next illustration shows the autoplastic experiences of form still more clearly, as by this time the boy had succeeded in clarifying his mode of representation. The wrinkles on the forehead are drawn like steps and clearly originate from a purely tactual experience received through the fingers gliding down the forehead. I say ' originally ' because during the actual process of drawing no control was exercised through the sense of touch. That would have been merely a disturbing influence and would have contradicted the autoplastic experience of muscular innervation. In other words the tactual experience of form has been incorporated into the consciousness of form without being controlled by visual perception. This interaction of tactual experience of form and autoplastic sensations of form produces a mode of representation characteristic of the haptic type. We must realise this if we wish to understand the mode of creativeness of this type, which we find in exactly the same form among the weak sighted.

Case 2. J. M., 18 years, weak sighted (cf. Table I, No. 6). He can read print and though his physical capacity would be sufficient to enable him to use his sight in drawing, he behaves exactly like a totally blind person. He can express himself by means of threedimensional modelling (Pl. 8), but is quite unable to find his way about on plane paper. The concept of a line as an abstraction is foreign to him and he is unable to conceive of drawing as a means of expression. His plastic work shows all the characteristics of that of a fully blind person. He uses his eyes only when external circumstances force him to do so. He never looks at his completed models but feels them over, although he would be quite able to scrutinise them with his eyes. This way of working, without making use of vision although the physical capacity is present, is typical and always occurs where inner tendencies towards visual creativeness are absent.

The opposite case to this would be that of a blind person whose talent is visual. It is necessary to investigate separately those who were born blind or became blind at an early age and those who became blind at a later age. Those who become blind later naturally have associations and visual memory images of objects, though we shall of course expect to find among them also cases whose orientation was non-visual even while they were able to see. The problem is much more interesting in the case of those who were blind at birth or went blind at an early age.

In his chapter on the creative types Ludwig Münz [1] discusses three stages in creative work. First, " pseudo naturalistic representation " in which the apprehension of particulars is still rather diffuse and necessarily rather generalised. The individual representatives of gesture, though present in rudimentary form, are not yet completely clarified. Consequently this first stage seems to be closer to reality than the second, higher stage, that of " strictly structurated representation ". This is distinguished from the pseudo realistic stage by the clear structure and synthesis of the symbols representing individual parts. Within this stage the individual representative symbols of gesture and expression are gradually formulated and articulated more precisely and from being merely added together are built up into a structurally unified whole. The third stage is called by Münz the " stage of correspondence to reality ". This stage seems to a person with full sight, even if he does not know how it has been developed, the one in which the picture is in the widest sense identical with what is actually seen in space. As the various parts are essentially subordinate to the whole, our eyes receive an impression of a picture corresponding to external reality. Münz points out, however, that even the person who becomes blind later in life does not necessarily arrive at this realistic stage. From this he draws the incorrect inference that it is the *talent* with which a person has been born that decisively determines whether or not he will reach the stage of realistic correspondence in the case of tactual forms. But this inference needs to be corrected, as more or less imperfect realistic tactual forms are produced also by the untalented, that is, by those whose aptitudes have remained stereotype and who have not achieved more than a limited measure of technical ability to express their experiences. It is not hereditary or acquired

[1] *Op. cit.*

talent which is decisive but, as our previous investigations have shown, the *creative type*, the absorption in one or other of the worlds of sensory experience. There are blind or weak sighted people, and even, as we have shown, certain types with normal vision, who never experience the need of achieving that unified form which Münz describes as " corresponding to reality ". Then, again, there are those whose most striking characteristic is the desire to achieve a total unified form. The former are the haptic type and the latter the visual type. Pl. 9 shows a model by H. St. who had been blind since birth. Its very title, " The Longing For Sight," is characteristic of her visual type. It shows particularly clearly how ' tactual form ' and ' tactual concept ' have fused into that unified whole which Ludwig Münz calls the " stage of correspondence with reality ".[1] Equally characteristic of both creative types are their totally different modes of imaging. P. H., who has been blind since birth and belongs to the haptic type (Pl. 68) says, " I have my work before me in my imagination as though I could grasp it. When I think of it I imagine to myself how the different parts would *feel*." It is important to note that the act of touch is connected with his images even after a piece of work has been completed. A visual type such as H. St., on the other hand, has no need for such an imaginary act of touch. She thinks of a model without imagining herself touching it.

The investigation of the preceding cases shows clearly that the two types which I have called the visual type and the haptic type are creative types, and that independently of the physical possibilities of sight, they feel and express their world of experience in terms of their own fundamental categories.

[1] O. Wulff speaks of ' visual form ' and ' visual concept '. Münz's terms, ' tactual form ' and ' tactual concept ' are the corresponding ones for the sense of touch. *Vide* footnote, p. 3.

CHAPTER VI

AN ANALYSIS OF THE DRAWINGS OF WEAK SIGHTED PUPILS

(a) THE PICTORIAL REPRESENTATION OF 'HAPTIC SPACE'

Space cannot be conceived in its totality. Its infinity is irrational and it becomes accessible to our senses only when we circumscribe it. At the centre of space, with nothing whatever to surround us, space itself would be infinite and therefore non existent. The self would cease to be a measure of value in space. It would vanish to nothing in infinity. Our senses set limits to space and each in its own way enables us to grasp it. Visual space, for which the eyes are the intermediaries, we perceive as the widest space. Haptic space, for which our organs of touch and our bodily sensations are the intermediaries, as the most restricted. Both spaces achieve a magical significance whenever the self is included in them through value judgments. In what follows we shall discuss the difference in the way in which these two sensory spaces are pictorially represented. The direction of our investigation is determined on the one hand by the difference in the modes of sensory perception of these two spaces, and on the other, by the restriction of the extent of haptic space as compared with visual space.

In relation to its environment the self grows or diminishes both in size and in importance. Next to children we seem large, next to a cathedral, small ; unimportant in the world at large, important in our own circle ; most important, perhaps, when we are quite alone. These attitudes vary according to our psychological state. The narrower, the more restricted threedimensional space or the space of our psychological experiences is, the more importance we assign to the self. Haptic space is of necessity restricted. It is determined both as regards its extent and its modes of perception by the immediate and the wider touch space. In it, therefore, the significance and the importance of the self are very much emphasised. The effect of the importance of the self on the perception of space as well as on its pictorial representation will be discussed in what follows.

In the visual image produced by the eye differences show themselves by, among other properties, the apparent diminution of distant objects. In drawing, this apparent diminution of distant objects is achieved by using laws of perspective. The outer limits of visual space are represented by the boundary of the horizon line. How are distant objects represented in haptical space? Distant objects do not produce differences in size to the sense of touch. Thus the visual image receives its first decisive correction. When space is being explored tactually, distances can only have different values attached to them or seem of greater or less importance. Haptic space, therefore, is one in which we find a predominance of subjective judgments of value. The perspective of touch is a perspective of values. Objects behind one another are represented as next to one another or above one another; this we know from the earliest beginnings of spatial representation. The conceptions of children and of primitive peoples are not visual but are to a high degree bound up with the self. We shall therefore expect to find close parallels which we shall discuss in greater detail in the final chapter.

As we are concerned with the pictorial representation of haptic space I shall begin at the point at which it is possible to distinguish clearly between the spatial conceptions of the two creative types. I shall therefore not discuss the first stages of spatial representation, which are to be found in the drawings of children, but merely remind the reader of the important fact that the drawings of all types have a common origin. From this we conclude that *the specific nature of the two types shows itself only at a later stage of development* and we shall now proceed to determine this stage more precisely.

(1) *Linear Representation*

The first method of organising space, which must be considered as the beginning of a 'touch perspective', is to represent by means of lines built one on top of the other, the idea of things being behind each other (Pl. 10). Their limits are strictly defined and for every spatial zone a new line is drawn which creates a new basis.[1]   The drawing shown in Pl. 10 was made by a child of fourteen. Compared with the work of normal children of his own age his drawing belongs to a much earlier age, that is, it is apparently retarded. But as it was the starting point of his drawing activity it indicates the possibilities which at that time, his thinking about space had. Because the intelligence of the blind is fully matured their plastic work develops in a series of jumps from the most primitive to a highly developed stage of representation. So in this pupil we can trace a rapid succession of ontogenetic developmental stages (compare, for instance, the developmental series, Pls. 15 and 16). The subject of the drawing is a street. The figures are all the same size and have been placed next to each other without any differentiated movement. No figure is obscured by any other because that does not correspond to the thought processes of this type. Intersections would indicate that objects are behind each other in space and that is confined to visual space perception.[2] The lamps in the shop windows like the clocks have been built over each other. This drawing is typical and is one of many drawings, all at the same stage of development, by this particular type.

Pl. 10*b* shows a school on fire. The pupils are rushing in wild disorder out of the burning building. In this drawing two characteristic properties of this type and of his particular stage of development can be seen with particular clarity : movement, and the fact that individual figures are behind one another. The articulation of space beyond the principle of the base line is not yet possible. The individual persons are all oriented towards the base line. Nevertheless the fact of their being behind one another has been represented, though it has been facilitated by the chaotic movement of

---

[1] We know this line from children's drawings as the ' base line ', and, when drawing has become more conscious, it attains a greater importance.

[2] In the drawing of haptic space there can thus be no overlappings as there are in the drawing of perspective.

the crowd. When I enquired why the gateway had been left empty, or rather why only one unfinished figure had been put in it, he answered that otherwise one would not be able to see that those people were not like the ones in front but had to come *out of* the gateway. In other words, although this is not a solution of the problems of the representation of threedimensional space, it nevertheless gives a first indication that the problem has been recognised. If Sch. Gr. had completed the figure his intention of showing that it was coming out of the gateway would have conflicted with the actual facts of the drawing in which the emerging figure would then have appeared in the same plane as the others. Therefore he preferred to leave it incomplete. This empty portion is psychologically one of the most important parts of the drawing. It shows for the first time the desire to draw depth and this indicates that we are here dealing with a visual type.

(2) *The Mixture of Plan and Elevation as a Means of Articulating Space*

At later stages the mixture of the two projections as a means of representing threedimensional space is typical.

Pl. 11, people on sleighs, shows this mixture of the two projections particularly clearly (cf. figs. 54 *a* and *b*). The sleigh was an object with which the pupil was intimately acquainted. He had handled and used it often and therefore felt it essential to show all the parts that were known to him, the seat as well as the two runners. The obvious solution was to choose a drawing in plan, which enabled him to represent both seat and runners. Bent legs, he felt, were characteristic of the sensation of sitting. These, however, are most clearly seen when a side elevation drawing is made. In order to harmonise these two projections he connected them by means of a conceptual act : he placed the feet on the runners. By mixing these two projections he created a kind of space although from our point of view it suffers from an inner disharmony.

(3) *The Further Constructive Development of the Representation of Space*

Pls. 53*b* and 54 show in what way the double aspect develops into a single aspect, provided the artist's orientation is visual. The subject for drawing was swans swimming. All the pupils naturally drew the pond in bird's-eye view. This was then bounded by grasses which were drawn diametrically away from the bank. The pond had now been given a sharply defined boundary.[1] Notice that this boundary is also the base line for the grasses. To draw an island in the middle of the pond was easy. But when they were asked to draw a tree on this island opinions began to diverge. One group used the boundary of the island as a base line for the tree, which they drew upwards as far as the next boundary (Pl. 54). The other group got into difficulties about this conception. A tree naturally grows upwards. " Well, but then it would lie in the pond," was one of the objections raised, until one of them said " I shall let the tree grow up beyond the pond ". He followed my advice and first drew the swans. Then he noticed that the tree which he drew later half covered one of his swans, and so brought up the whole problem of visual space. " I see, the tree covers the swan just as when I hold my hand before my face and hide one finger behind it ! " I observed that only the second group imitated this exercise and was delighted at the discovery. The first group was quite uninterested and completed its drawings in its own fashion.

Pl. 12 shows skaters on the ice. Only a visual type could have achieved this free representation of space in which the determination by fixed base lines has been abandoned. Here the proportions of the human figures and the trees are of interest. They indicate that the human figure has greater value and this particular kind of value emphasis is common to both weak sighted types. Pls. 13 *a* and *b* show a woman

---

[1] The desire to impose boundaries, intelligible because it makes space easier to grasp through touch, is also to be found in the plastic work of the blind. The narrower the boundaries are, the more easily can they be apprehended through touch. Consequently the imposition of boundaries is characteristic of this type.

gathering wood in a forest. Here again, though not quite so distinctly, we see that the trees have been grouped around the figure. They thus make the figure into the central point and also define its space in a similar manner to the definition of the space of the pond. But a new factor has now come into experience : the conscious realisation of the vastness of the forest. This is particularly intense here because it can be perceived neither visually nor tactually and must remain unknown. It becomes clear only through the fact that the size of the human figure is negligible compared to that of the forest. At this stage of development, at which space and form are consciously experienced, the differentiation between the experience of space by the visual and haptic type occurs. For the visual types the problems of the surrounding space continue to be of importance. For the haptic types, on the other hand, they disappear and instead are replaced in the drawings by a strongly expressive value emphasis on subjective experiences.

(4) *The Articulation of Space Considered as a Direct Consequence of Physical Defect*

We shall now have to consider separately the perception and the representation of space in the case of visual and haptic types. It should be emphasised once again that when we speak of the visual type we have in mind the restricted visual type, whose visual acuity is restricted by a physical defect. What is characteristic of this type is that it has the impulse to draw and to model as though it possessed full vision. Put another way, where full vision is lacking there is nevertheless a desire to transform haptic impressions into optical impressions. The optical experience even when it has been ' intended ' as such is only apparently an optical experience. This is shown by the fact that tactual impressions are often valued in a different way from optical impressions. Because the impulse to translate tactual experiences into optical experiences is conscious, the drawing tends to be an intellectual construction. This constructional method of ' seeing ' and drawing can be seen in small objects as well as on a large scale in the representation of space. Pl. 14*a* is a drawing of flowers. Sch. G. inspected the flowers closely with his eye in order to get the optical impression demanded by his type. Having given them a superficial visual inspection he proceeded to draw fig. 1. The one sided view presented to his eye had probably led him to consider that there were several petals. He then drew fig. 2, but perceived neither the number nor the arrangement of the individual petals. He once again brought the flower closely before his eyes and convinced himself that because of his high visual defect, which for all practical purposes is equivalent to blindness, he was unable to achieve an impression of the flower as a whole. He therefore turned the flower and studied the arrangement of the petals. Fig. 3 proves that the act of turning, that is, letting the individual petals go past his eye, resulted in his placing them next to each other in the drawing. This arrangement did not satisfy him, since it did not express the ' roundness ', an impression of which he had got whilst turning the flower. He therefore drew fig. 4, in which we can see the influence of the act of turning. Finally, after he had further investigated the flower tactually and by tearing them off satisfied himself that there were a number of petals, he drew them in the correct circular order in fig. 5. After a further visual examination he found that his tactual impression completely corresponded with the optical impression and thereby all further restrictions on his drawing were removed. I then took the spray away from him and he produced Pl. 14*b*, which is as it were a mental synthesis of his visual and tactual experiences and is incomparably more forceful, less concerned with considerations of reality, a far freer representation.

We see, then, that the optical experience of space has been constructed out of numerous tactual experiences which by a mental act have been fused together into a single image. The typical example of the degree to which the experience of a spatial whole has to be constructed is shown in Pl. 33. Sch. G. can never have a visual impression which remotely resembles his painting. A reference to Table 1 shows that he is practically blind. How then could he produce such a large scale painting of an accident? Obviously the 'accident', of which there is hardly anything to be seen accurately in the middle foreground, was merely a means to an end. He wished to have some reason for the many lights which seemed to him necessary as fixation marks for his orientation. So he strung together masses of motor cars and trams that had been blocked by the accident. These gave him the possibility of, as it were, feeling his way along from one light to the other and of in this way constructing his picture space. This was the only way in which he could have achieved a unified effect.

The previous investigations can now be summarised as follows.

(1) The beginnings of spatial representation, visual as well as haptic, are the same.

(2) The development of the individual creative type occurs when the shape and magnitude of space have become a conscious experience and are consciously represented.

(3) The haptic representation of space is more closely bound up with the self, that is, with subjective experiences and value judgments.

(4) The representation of space by a restricted visual type is constructional. It introduces value judgments only when some relation to the self is expressed. Nevertheless it contains all the properties that lead to the concept of perspective in space.

(b) THE AUTOPLASTIC EXPERIENCE OF FORM

Just as the representation of haptic space is intermixed with subjective value judgments, so the pictorial representation of gestures and expressions starts from personal experience, from the autoplastic experience of form. The self is projected as the true actor of the picture the formal characteristics of which are the resultant of a synthesis of bodily and intellectual apprehension of shape and expression. We shall proceed to analyse these subjective experiences and their expression in the form of pictures in order to reveal the general creative basis and principles of this particular type of artist.

(1) *The Development of the Primitive Outline*

The mental act that takes place when a concept or an image is projected in the form of a drawing or picture consists in a continual addition or subtraction of symbols for form and expression to or from a primitive outline. This primitive outline, which is the starting point of the drawing, is from the beginning closely bound up with the end product. By primitive outline I understand that shape or figure serving as the framework for the addition of symbols of form and expression. That some image of the whole is present from the very beginning can be inferred, for example, from the long drawn out form of the primitive outline of a man crying out (Pl. 21) or the round form given to the primitive outline of a well set person, and so on. This primitive outline, which is to be the frame work of the expressive content of the drawing, changes according to the intention of the artist. Since it serves as the framework for the expressive experience of form it is a subjective element and at the same time an objective element in the constructive processes. The more strongly the artistic unity of the picture has become an experience of the artist, the more intense his bodily experiences, the clearer will be the articulation of the primitive outline (cf. the developmental series, Pl. 16). Whenever the original conception was not clear enough to result in a perfectly determinate form changes are made in the outline during the processes of drawing. The individual symbols of expression are added according to the importance of the expressions which they symbolise. The primitive outline is thus not merely the starting point but becomes the framework for all symbols of form and expression and is closely integrated with them. It is, therefore, in the truest sense of the word, a *mask*.

(2) *The Synthetic Mode of Representation*

When a blind person models, he usually shapes every element of form and expression separately before combining it with the primitive outline and assigning to it its true significance in relation to other symbols. In the case of drawing, however, the separation, addition or combination of the individual symbols for form and expression can itself be carried out merely symbolically, as the symbols cannot be taken out of the plane of the paper. Nevertheless, before the haptic type proceeds to draw a picture, he separates out by means of a mental act the individual vehicles of expression and the form symbols in order to perceive and understand them fully. He achieves the higher perception of the form as a whole only by attending to its individual parts. This process is undoubtedly connected with the fact that the objects of the more immediate tactual space are more easily perceived. Only when the separate parts have been incorporated in the primitive outline do the experiences concerned with separate forms become fused into an experience of the picture as a whole and only then is the true significance of the symbols seen. Looked at in this way, the reason why ridges and depressions are indicated in the same manner, by darker colours, becomes intelligible. Both are additions to the primitive outline or rather a ' filling ' of this outline. In Pl. 21, " The Cry for Help," the hollowness of the cheeks exists only in thought. Actually they have been ' added ' as independent symbols of form just as, for instance, the nose is added as a projecting part. Both have been given a darker colour. The same treatment of projections and depressions is seen even more clearly in the picture of an old woman (Pl. 25). Projecting chin and hollow cheeks have been symbolised in the same way. It is sometimes doubtful whether the shading indicates a projection or a hollow, particularly when pure formal symbols have been chosen to represent some particular expression. For instance, the temples vary in size according to the significance attached to them (cf. the developmental series of Pl. 16). We expect the colouring here to indicate a depression, but a glance at Pl. 58 shows that temples considered as formal symbols are thought of as projections. In other words the darker colour has nothing to do with shadows or other effects of visual space. Only things such as dark or light hair, or the colour of the lips, can indirectly be traced to optical impressions, though even here the conceptual element may predominate. The grey colour of the hair has been thought of not so much as colour but rather as a symbol for age.

This survey of the synthetic mode of working leads us to the important conclusion that *dark and light colours refer to visual impressions only when the nature of the colour is directly determined by the nature of the object.*

(3) *The Structure of the Visual Representative Symbols of Expression*

The clearer and more distinct the consciousness of form, the more intense the experience of shape, the more definite becomes the articulation of individual symbols. The first stage in the drawing of an expressive mask shows that there is as yet no clear differentiation of individual lineaments (cf. the developmental series, Pl. 16, figs. 1 and 2). The consciousness of form is vague, the language of form confused, although the effect of the picture as a whole indicates that there had been a vivid experience of shape. In Pl. 17, which follows the series of Pl. 16 and is by the same haptic pupil, we cannot yet speak of individual lineaments the structure of which has been thoroughly worked out. They are blurred and yet in this rather unclear mode of representation make an apparently better naturalistic impression than in succeeding stages. This particular stage of drawing has a close parallel in the plastic work of the blind,[1] and is called by Münz the ' pseudo-naturalistic stage '. The undifferentiated forms of the individual representatives of expression when taken as a whole give an impression that seems close to reality. Although at this stage the symbols for eyes, mouth, and nose are already present in their typical forms, they are not portrayed clearly but show that consciousness of form is as yet rather vague. Even Pl. 18 still belongs to the same stage. Although there is a greater number of expressive symbols such as wrinkles on the forehead and cheeks, so that the primitive outline seems more ' filled ', the total impression is still confused. The individual representative symbols

[1] In *Plastische Arbeiten Blinder*, Münz has demonstrated this mode of working in the congenitally blind.

of expression have not yet received a clear structural formulation. Consequently the language of form seems confused and its expression vague. This is most clearly shown by the confused treatment of the folds on the cheeks. The translation of muscular and bodily sensations into the language of forms is still difficult because attempts at the pictorial representation of autoplastic experiences of form are as yet absent or, at best, vague.

Then comes the great experience : the step to conscious apprehension (Pl. 19, fig. 3, of the developmental series). At first sight we suspect that there has been a regression, that the living form has become a petrefact. Actually, however, we are dealing with an intensification of the consciousness of individual muscular and bodily sensations. The language of forms becomes as clear as possible. It is no longer sufficient to put down merely the shape of the nose. In order to make it as distinct as possible it is surrounded by a line to emphasise its structure. Again when the mouth and teeth are drawn, the urge to define the forms as clearly as possible goes so far that the drawings become mechanised, to the detriment of expressiveness. This ' mechanisation '—drawing the teeth in rows, circumscribing the nose by means of a line, the factual emphasis of the eyes—is not a mere external mechanical matter but is typical of this particular stage. It expresses a definite consciousness of form. What was confused has become ordered ; what was a matter of feeling and intuition has become a matter for conscious creation. The inflexibility of the drawing is determined from within, by the creative process itself. The experience of form has not been arrested, but a new starting point for further work has been created.

The following pictures in this developmental series all belong to the third stage, which is characterised by the fact that the individual symbols for form and expression are now integrated with the experience of the shape as a whole in order to achieve a pictorial unity. The individual representative symbols of expression are clearly recognizable as such ; we have no difficulty in isolating them from the primitive outline ; nevertheless they do fuse with it into a formal whole. The schematic aspect of the picture has completely disappeared. For every lineament a new representative symbol is made, the form and expression of which can change. Only certain symbols keep on recurring— the temple, a particular way of drawing a nostril. Even these are not entirely inflexible, but fit in with the whole facial expression. Only in the case of visual types could I observe that the isolation of individual symbols of form and expression disappeared and that a total form was achieved in which the individual symbols fused completely with the primitive outline and became unrecognizable as separate symbols (cf. Pl. 15).

To sum up : broadly speaking there are three stages in the progressive articulation of individual symbols of form and expression.

(1) Because it is not yet possible to translate muscular sensations and the experience of shape into the forms of a drawing, there is no clear articulation either of the individual forms or of the picture as a whole and the picture remains confused.

(2) Sensations and feelings about forms become conscious and the synthetic or constructional mode of working becomes dominant. This gives the impression that the drawing as a whole is rigid and frequently schematic.

(3) The consciousness of form and the experience of the unity of perception are fused together. At this stage the symbols of the different parts are strongly differentiated, but though we can still isolate them they nevertheless subordinate themselves to the picture as a whole. The picture is therefore strongly expressive and clearly shows the symbols of expression.

(4) *The Co-ordination of Affectively Toned Symbols for Form*

We have to pay particular attention to the manner and sequence of the co-ordination of these symbols. The level of articulation reached in the development of the individual symbols decides the manner in which they are co-ordinated in the drawing, because the structural level is closely related to the possibility of experiencing a perceptual whole.   In the first stages, in which feeling and consciousness of form are still vague, the individual representative symbols of form and expression are merely placed next to one another.   This manner of drawing corresponds to the spatial thought processes and images of this stage and is succeeded later by a stage at which the different forms are drawn above one another. The procedure is very similar to that of the blind when modelling. The blind first model the eye by making a cavity and placing a ball in it. Only later do they proceed to the more complicated form : the eyes lying in their sockets and having eyelids pulled over them. In a similar fashion the weak sighted first draw the eye or the pupil within an oval, at a later stage they prepare the socket by means of a darker colour, over which the eye with the pupil is painted, later still the eyes are supplied with eyelids. The thought processes are similar in all cases : the eye is ' put into ' its socket. This superposition of different strata is characteristic of the more advanced stages and is closely related to the way in which thinking and imaging proceed. The world is not so much perceived as an external object, but is built up from within and coloured by the artist's own emotional experiences.

The individual representatives of form and expression are co-ordinated within a picture at different times. Certain shapes are drawn first for reasons of orientation. In Pl. 22 nose and eyebrows were drawn first though as a matter of fact in this case affective reasons as well as the need for orientation played a part. The various representative symbols for expression are placed according to their emotional significance. In order to give a clear picture of the creative processes and the way in which the individual symbols for form and expression are co-ordinated in the drawing, it will be well to study the genesis of an expressive mask. Let us turn our attention to Pl. 21, " The Cry For Help."

The starting point, as for every drawing of a head, was the simple elliptic outline to which other parts were added in the order of their affective importance. The drawn up eyebrows and the widely opened mouth were put in first.

for in them the greatest tension is felt. The tremendous tension between eyes and mouth is probably the most important bodily experience when screaming. This tension, as the drawing clearly shows, starts at the cheekbone just below the eyes and as a purely subjective autoplastic sensation can be felt as a strong pull downward from the nose. This has been depicted with clarity and certainty by the two symbols of expression running from the nose and eyes downwards towards the jaw and round the mouth. It is a not unreasonable analogy to compare the sensation of stretching with that of an elastic band, which, like the 'bands of pathos' in the drawing, narrows towards the middle. This tremendous autoplastic experience dominates the whole head. 'Tension' in the truest sense of the word is brought into the gesture, and its expressive content is heightened by the eyes squinting with horror. The hollowness of the cheeks is indicated by a dark colour as though the artist wished to take something away from the cheeks. This darker shade must be regarded as a shadow. It is a purely synthetic symbol of 'taking away', that is, it is the symbol for a hollow. The black wide open nostrils which have been especially emphasised below the nose, are also particularly important as symbols of expression. The nose has been only partially circumscribed and therefore stands out mainly by contrast with the surrounding shapes, although in accordance with the synthetic mode of procedure it, too, has been 'added' as an independent part by means of a darker tone. The wrinkles of the forehead have not been differentiated much and have been treated more as a whole because they do not give rise to clear separate sensations. The ears which have also been added to the head clearly show lines that represent touch impressions. The two ridges are parallel as they would appear to the fingers drawn along the ear itself. Again corresponding to the sense of touch the opening has been placed in the centre of the ear. The head is finished off with the wildly disordered hair. Also of importance are the shoulders, which have been drawn up in fear. The button, which as H. A. says, is to indicate that the coat has also been raised and therefore seems to him to be important, has only just found room between the chin and the edge of the paper.

We must therefore conclude that the autoplastic experience of form and its pictorial expression are intimately bound up in the images of *all* those whose orientation is haptic. This conclusion justifies us in inferring the closest parallel to the creative processes of primitive peoples, with which we shall be concerned in a later chapter.

NOTE.—In *Plastische Arbeiten Blinder* by Münz and Lowenfeld, Münz maintains that autoplastic drawing strongly indicates that bodily sensations are the primary determinant of the spatial conceptions and images of people who have been born blind or who have become blind at an early age. The investigations which have just been discussed showed that this statement has to be extended so as to include all those whose primary concern is with haptic experience, also normal sighted people who are primarily haptic.

(c) THE SIGNIFICANCE OF COLOUR

(1) *The Phase of Decorative Colour*

Among the first visual perceptions are those of colour. The visual impressions of the weak sighted are at first mostly indeterminate, but unless the organic defect is too severe they can be trained to achieve very fine distinctions. The investigations which follow began after this training had been achieved and will concern themselves with the significance of colour in the development of the art of the weak sighted.

The first coloured pictures show that even in the case of the weak sighted the rhythmical element is as predominant as it is in the beginning of linear drawings. The first drawings are determined neither by the importance nor by the localised qualities of colour. Colours are placed next to one another simply from a feeling for rhythm and in this way the first decorative basis is laid. Pl. 12 " Skaters ", is a typical example of this mode of painting. Colour is used here quite freely without reference to particular objects, from a simple instinctive delight in the colours themselves. A closer inspection, however, shows that the arrangement of colours is not entirely arbitrary but has rhythmic influences. We see that darker and lighter colours recur with a certain periodicity and this may be the basis for the obvious impression of unity given by the picture. For the naïve taste uninfluenced by training, the problem of consciously harmonising colours does not arise. There is nothing new in the reflection that the later work of normal children is frequently influenced by tastes and fashions of the day. But we shall see that the development of colour in the work of weak sighted children remains uninfluenced by external tendencies and conventions and goes its own way. The colour effects are frequently particularly subtle ; but we shall discover an increasing tendency to harmonise conceptually the forms with the colours assigned to them.

(2) *The Stage of Object Colours*

" The bark of a tree is brown ; the leaves are green." This linguistic formulation rules thinking at a certain level and dominates the next stage, that of conceptual object colours. For a brief period the colour impulses of the weak sighted are suppressed by *knowledge* about the colours of objects. But it would be quite wrong to believe that because the weak sighted are more isolated from their environment they regard this way of assigning colours as their own. To a far greater degree than in the case of the normal sighted their world is a world of appearances. As they are more isolated from their environment, their consciousness of self is more highly developed and therefore the stage in which it is recognised that colours are assignable to objects is merely a transition to the stage at which their own world of appearances is again put first. On the one hand we have the environment and its colour effects ; on the other subjective bodily experiences. When the latter are projected in the form of a picture, colour becomes one of the most important symbols of expressiveness.

As regards the significance of colour, therefore, we again see how different are the conceptions of the two creative types. The visual type is concerned with colour *impressions*, whilst the haptic type uses colour in a more symbolic way as a means of *expression*.

(3) *The Realistic Reproduction of Colour*

Objects at a distance from the eye of the weak sighted are blurred not only with regard to their form but also their colour. It is true, as Pl. 17 shows, that the light of the setting sun delights the artist, but it is direct light which falls into his eye. The tree in the foreground seems to him dark and shadowy. It is not possible for him to make colour distinctions here. The ability to make them, as we shall show, develops from mental processes unconnected with the processes of sight. It follows that silhouettes at first play an important part in drawings by the weak sighted, for everything at some distance from the eye appears shadowy, that is ' dark ', particularly when the background is bright. This gives us a new way of dealing with the concept of colour, but in this case it is found not in the conceptual object but directly from visual experience. The tree is therefore painted black (Pl. 17). Black here simply means ' dark ', ' shadowy '. But a closer inspection of Pls. 12 and 15 shows clearly that the painting of colours in space develops. In the earlier picture the colour of objects at different distances is the same, the tree in the foreground is treated in the same way as the background. But in Pl. 27 we see that near and distant objects are treated differently. The trees in the foreground appear shadowy and are therefore painted black, but in the distance they again receive their local colour. This means that *when there is no longer any possibility of obtaining a visual impression, objects are painted in the colours they are known to have.* So long as trees can affect the eyes of the weak sighted it is their sensory impression with which he is concerned. When, however, a tree lies in regions inaccessible to his sight it ceases to be a sensible appearance and becomes an object, ' tree as such,' tree with a brown bark and green leaves. The colours in this region of the painting therefore are those of conceptual knowledge and not of sensible appearance.

Gradually, however, the reciprocal relation between what is depicted and what is experienced leads to an autonomous treatment of colour that is applied also to the immediate environment. Sch. G. has painted houses in very different settings, in sunshine (Pl. 51), at night (Pl. 40), and so on, and the colour has been related to the mood as a whole. We stand before a miracle when we see Sch. G. at work. His eyes are extremely close to the paper and he follows bodily even the smallest stroke of his brush because he is not able to see two things next to each other. Nevertheless, he achieves a unified picture. We cannot understand this in any other way than by realising that the coloured picture as a whole is present to his mind. Only in this way can we understand the astonishing unity achieved by the numerous partial impressions whose synthesis reproduces the picture he has in mind. The boy in whom the physical ability to see has been restricted to the barest minimum, who is practically blind, achieves this miraculous effect of ' natural vision '. It is a triumph of the spirit, which has transcended his defect and has enabled him to express without hindrance that of which nature has denied him sensory experience. He has, through the power of his work, entered into the birthright that was denied him.

(4) Colour as an Expressive Symbol

We tend to say that symbols are the more ' arbitrary ' the less they agree with our own experience or the less direct comparison is possible between our visual impressions of reality and a picture. The particular way in which symbols have been assigned ceases to be arbitrary, however, when we understand the experience that has led to it. The representative symbols of haptic form and expression, the origin of which is tactual or which spring from various personal bodily experiences, are as little arbitrary as are the representative symbols of direct visual experience. For the haptic creative type we can distinguish two ways of expressing the significance of colour. Colour may be assigned to an object on the basis of an immediate sense impression, or it may be assigned according to some set of rules. Only in the latter case do we speak of colour symbolism.

It seems strange to connect colour with haptic experiences.

We must therefore be all the more concerned to investigate its meaning and the significance of its usage. Let us investigate colour in some concrete cases, the expressive masks by H. A. What for him is the significance of the colour of his primitive outlines? On the one hand, he certainly chose colour simply to provide a material basis for his further work; on the other, we have to ask why it is yellow in one case and brown, green or pink in another. This use of colour undoubtedly has a conceptual origin, as is clearly shown by the fact H. A. paints the face of a man quivering with fright (Pl. 23) green or says that the yellow face is 'pale'. In other words, the expression "quivering with fear" seems to him to necessitate a green face, which surely has not been derived from a visual experience. In popular speech an angry man is said to "spit gall", and this may account for H.'s choice of green.

If we examine the colours of individual representative symbols of expression we shall find that they are not constant but are adapted to the colour of the picture as a whole. Nevertheless we shall find that the colour of individual symbols is sometimes determined by a constant relationship between the colour and the experience or feeling it expresses. I found, for example, that there was a tendency to stereotype the colour only of certain individual parts such as the temples, the nostrils, and so on.

As regards the actual colours themselves we have to note that they are not determined by visual impressions. This is quite clear from the fact that elevations and depressions are treated in the same way, a treatment which was discussed in detail above.

(5) *Summary*

Let us sum up what has been said about the colour experiences of the weak sighted. Colour is the first thing that the weak sighted can experience through his eyes. In his pictures we can distinguish three stages in the use of colour.

(i) The *decorative stage*, which is determined entirely by considerations of colour rhythm.

(ii) At the second stage, *colour is related to objects*, that is, the colour assigned is that of ' local colour ' or known colour.

(iii) The third stage differs in the case of the two types. The *visual type* achieves a realistic colour correspondence. That is, the colours vary according to the influence of light, atmosphere, or mood. Intermediate to this stage is one at which objects inaccessible to sensory perception are drawn according to the artist's knowledge of their local colour. The *haptic type* on the other hand, directs the use of his colour conceptually or through a system of colour symbolism.

(*d*) THE RELATIONSHIP BETWEEN THE ART OF THE BLIND AND THAT OF THE WEAK SIGHTED

The blind build up their conceptions out of individual elements each of which has been apprehended through the sense of touch.   Out of these elements they construct a synthesis of appearances. In the same way, according to the kind and degree of their weak sightedness, the weak sighted build up their conceptions out of visual or tactual partial impressions. This is true, however, only for the reproduction of the forms as a whole. Those weak sighted subjects whose orientation is visual are helped in achieving their concept of the whole by visual impressions, however shadowy and uncertain these may be, while those whose orientation is haptic make no use of such impressions. In both cases, however, the relation of their creative processes to those of the blind is clear because neither group is able to achieve directly an impression of the whole, which is in all cases constructed out of separate partial impressions. The visual weak sighted type assimilates these partial impressions to his visual percept, however indefinite this may be and in this way gradually develops a structually more complete image. The haptic weak sighted type on the other hand, because his partial impressions are the same as they are for the blind, will approximate more closely to the haptic blind both as regards his conceptions as a whole and his creative output.

(1) ' *Constructive Seeing* ' *through the Summation of Touch Impressions*

A blind person models a head by first making a roughly spherical primitive outline. In this he hollows out the eye sockets, models the eyes separately, puts them into the sockets, and only then puts eyelids over them. In other words the bust is modelled not according to its surface characteristics, but is built up from within. In the same way he makes the mouth cavity, then the line of the gums and the teeth, and only later adds the lips over them. One finds that the teeth are modelled even when the mouth is later closed.

The haptic weak sighted proceed in an exactly similar manner when they are drawing. Pl. 22 shows an incompleted head. Here too, the simple primitive outline was prepared first. After the eye sockets had been painted in a darker colour the eyes were painted as white round discs, after which the eyelids were ' drawn ' over them. We thus see how similar the processes are. The blind in their models represent the eye by a hollow space into which a sphere is inserted, though naturally this is varied in various ways. In the drawings of certain types of weak sighted pupils the same thing happens. A dark circular space is created into which a white disc corresponding to the spherical eye is inserted. It must again be emphasised that in both these cases we are comparing similar creative types. The physiological differences play only a minor role. Pl. 29, by P. H who is congenitally blind, and Pl. 30 by G. S. who is weak sighted, provide striking illustrations of this fact. The subject for the bust and for the drawing is the same. It is important to remember that the darker colour represents both elevation and depression and indeed frequently means neither the one nor the other but is simply intended as a symbol, as for example in the case of the circular temples the colour of which merely indicates where they are supposed to be and what their size is (cf. Pls. 20–26). Exactly the same thing can be found in the plastic work of the blind. In Pl. 58 for instance, the wart-like protuberances at the sides are intended to represent the temples. It is quite clear that in the drawing (Pl. 30) G. S. had before him a conception of the whole, as his picture is based on the fact that one side of the face is distorted because it is leaning on the hand. In other words, when G. S. drew the primitive outline of the head he already signified that the autoplastic experience of the cheek resting on the hand had been clearly envisaged by him. Here, too, the achievement of a unified impression is essentially dependent upon the subjective experiences that find their expression in the drawing. Supporting the cheek was an experience confined to one side of the face and this has produced the asymmetry of the head. Within the head we find exactly the same symbols of expression as in the bust. We can see clearly how the sockets had been prepared in a darker colour for the reception of the eye and the pupil and that the eyelids were added last. Typical of autoplastic experience in both illustrations is the deep line leading from the root of the nose to the corners of the mouth. For visual perception these lines start at the nostrils (cf. also Pls. 31 and 59). Pl. 29 is taken from the book by Münz and Löwenfeld, *Plastische Arbeiten Blinder*, in which Münz gives a more detailed discussion of such expressive symbols of autoplastic experience. Especially instructive in the light it throws on this experience is the 'detached' cheek, which has been added as an independent symbol. The distortion of the cheek in Pl. 30 has produced the distortion of the mouth in which the teeth were added later. It is unusual to make such an addition later, but as we shall see there is a very good reason for it. Anatomically, of course, the teeth should still be horizontal even though the cheeks and lips have been drawn upwards. But the fact that the shape of the head is also distorted in the drawing already shows that the visual shape is of very minor importance. If, then, G. S. had drawn the teeth before he had drawn the lips he would not have been able to show in the same way that according to his sensations the mouth as a whole is also distorted and drawn upwards. It appears, therefore, that by putting in the teeth afterwards he resolved the conflict which would otherwise have occurred if he had drawn them first and then painted the lips over them. It is quite clear that his bodily sensations determined the shapes in this picture. A further important point to notice is that the tendons of the hand have been separately imposed as formal symbols. This manner of representation also finds its complete parallel in the plastic work of the haptic blind.

(2) *Simultaneity*

One difficulty in the examination of creative types is that one is inclined to attribute a greater importance than they actually have to differences in physical visual acuity. In order to make more accurate comparisons possible, therefore, let us confine ourselves to those weak sighted cases in which the physical defect is too great to allow any visual apprehension of shapes within the wider touch space other than the mere presence of some confused shadows. When we speak of the visual apprehension of a form, we have to distinguish clearly between the receptive processes and the processes of representation. The simultaneous perception of the different parts of an object is possible, for example, in the case of a nut which can be brought so closely before the eye that a clear picture is obtainable. We can compare this with the simultaneous apprehension of the same object by a blind person who in a single touch impression can perceive size, form and structure. Leaving aside for the moment the difficulties of representing raised and depressed forms, we may say that in the drawings the visual impression of a surface is reproduced in the same way as its actual impressions are reproduced in the case of models. Where the simultaneous visual apprehension of an object is not possible, however, for instance with objects in ' extended visual space ', individual impressions are built together, giving rise at first to an imperfect mental image which only gradually is constructed into a formal whole. The same thing happens in the case of the blind with respect to objects in ' extended tactual space '. In both cases, then, we see that a constructive synthesis of appearances is achieved which, from its very nature, must remain imperfect because this constructive mode of apprehending objects must be subject to emotional and value judgments. In both cases the perception of the form as a whole evolves in a temporal sequence and is not an instantaneous act.

The active processes that go to the making of a work of art depend very much upon the type of the artist. The haptic type arrives at some form of simultaneous image only through the working process, whilst the visual weak sighted type will in any situation construct his total impression out of numerous partial impressions. In other words, the presence of a unified conception in the case of the haptic type is determined by the fact that his experience of shape is intimately dependent on his autoplastic experiences. The visual weak sighted type on the other hand, allows his impressions to come to him from ' without ' and he is therefore not disturbed by the fact that they have to be constructed *a posteriori* out of numerous partial impressions. He will not, however, always be able to achieve a visual impression of the whole.

Pl. 32, " a Town by Night," illustrates this. Although the silhouettes of the houses have been ' correctly ' drawn, the lack of any sort of order among the lights shows a complete spatial disorientation such that even later it is not possible to bring the lights and the streets into relationship with one another. The simultaneity of the conception therefore essentially depends on the degree to which the picture has been intellectually apprehended. The rows of lights in the streets are not impressions that have come about as a result of a previous spatial orientation. They represent a kind of mental picture that is more in the nature of a feeling about the numerous streets in a city. Pl. 33, " Accident," shows that the disorder in the above picture is not owing to an incapacity to form a conception of spatial perspective. The artist has mastered all the difficulties of spatial representation and has created a picture in which the problems of space have been worked out to the last detail. This is because the whole space has been drawn into the orbit of his conception. The accident itself forms the centre : someone has been run over, the traffic has stopped, endless rows of cars and trams are unable to proceed. The problem here was properly to co-ordinate the endless lines of carriage lights. The artist solved it by ' feeling his way ' along from car to car and tram to tram, just as he would have done if he had actually had to find his way about. Only in this way was he able to give a ' correct ' spatial representation. By building up his picture out of numerous individual elements he was able to achieve that unified impression given by the picture. The picture has in effect brought the outer world closer to himself and is, as it were, a report of the events round about the artist, rather than a total conception which was present from the first.

Although the inner conditions are quite different, the same method of orientation, feeling one's way from one figure to another, can be seen in Pl. 34, " Moses bids farewell to his people." Here, too, space has been treated constructionally. As in earlier illustrations we see here the phenomenon of ' folding over '. At first sight the picture seems extremely schematic. A closer inspection shows, however, that the representation of each of the twelve tribes facing Moses has been accurately thought out. Even a kind of ' perspective ' can be recognized in the sense that all the figures are looking towards Moses. The first tribe has its back towards us and if we go round all twelve tribes we see that all of them are turned towards Moses, having him as their centre. Or, what is more relevant from the point of view of the picture, if we start from Moses we feel that he forms the centre and is attracting everything towards him. We are entitled to speak of " a kind of perspective " because the organization of this picture fixes the observer's line of vision in a definite direction. The inner determinants of this picture are very different from those discussed in the preceding paragraph. The exaggerated size of Moses, among other things, shows how strongly the artist is subjectively involved ; and this has *a priori* established the fact that the picture was conceived as a whole.

(3) *Overemphasis of Expressive Parts*

Pl. 35, " Youth Imploring," is a figure by a girl who has been blind since birth. Its most striking characteristic, which we feel to be closely connected with the title, is the overemphasis of the imploring hands. We feel the strength of the elemental forces embodied in this figure when we regard the gradual increase in its proportions. It starts from the slender basis of the delicate legs and rising like a hymn to heaven finds in the great hands its mighty closing chord. The base has, as it were, been dematerialised : it is no longer earth bound, and we have before us only the feeling " I implore ! "

In almost all the plastic work of the blind we find that those parts of the body that are emotionally emphasised are exaggerated. (Further examples can be found in the book by Münz and Löwenfeld, *Plastische Arbeiten Blinder*. For example the hand which is trying to retain the person who has said good-bye, Pl. 49 ; the heavy head of the sorrowing Odin, Pl. 46, etc.)

In the drawings of the weak sighted on the other hand, the various overemphases are fitted into the picture as a whole so as to harmonise with the general mode of presentation. It is more in accordance with the general nature of plastic art that the artist should start from the subjective experiences of his body and should subordinate his representations and their emotional overemphases wholly to his autoplastic experience of form. But in pictorial representation the artist's relation to his environment and his various attitudes to it will also play an important role. In Pls. 13 (*a*) and (*b*) for example, the effect of the greatness of the forest is enormously intensified when we perceive the size of the woman gathering wood. If the human figure were not there, the wood, instead of having an impressive greatness, would be reduced to an insignificant group of trees. When, however, the woman seeking wood becomes the centre of the picture (Pl. 36), the forest as such disappears and it is the figure of the old woman that makes itself immediately and strikingly felt. In Pl. 37 " Attack on a Public Building " the ' normal ' relationships have been maintained as long as the representation is schematically concerned with the crowd as a whole. Where, however, emotional significance is attributed to a figure this is very

K

much overemphasised. An instance of this is the person who has just fallen down dead. The same processes can be seen particularly well in Pl. 38, " Speaker." The crowd of people has been treated as a whole because they all have a common emotional attitude and the sizes of the various figures have been adapted to the size relationships of the picture. The speaker, however, seems to be floating above the crowd as a kind of over-dimensional spirit dominating and suppressing everything around him. A further excellent example is to be found in Pl. 39, " A Cripple crossing a Street is knocked down by a Motor Car." The cripple as the centre of the picture is overemphasised, and doubly overemphasised because of the special sympathy which he evokes. His hat and the coins he has lost being also important are also overemphasised. The obvious truth of our interpretation will be realized as soon as we compare the size of the cripple with that of the car which has knocked him down, the relation between the two exemplifying clearly the experience behind the picture. As a final characteristic example we may glance once more at Pl. 34, " Moses bidding farewell," in which this particular kind of value overemphasis is very clear. Moses is bidding farewell to his people and he appears, in a sense, as the idol of the people, for although he is showing himself in his human form, he is already transfigured as a god.

This type of picture, which is found in exactly the same form and with the same significance in miniatures of the early Middle Ages, will be discussed in greater detail in the last chapter. Here I should merely like to mention that in the *Kosmos Judikopleustes* we find a picture, " David and his Choirs," in which David as the centre of the choirs has been even more schematised and overemphasised.[1] In religious pictures of this kind we frequently find similar solutions of the problems of form and of organization to those in the drawings discussed above. Both are bound up with emotional experiences and not with the reproduction of visual images or impressions. Many more examples of this type of art could be discussed (cf. Pl. 75). However, as we are more

---

[1] Hermann Hieber, *Die Miniaturen des frühen Mittelalters.*

concerned with the principles according to which creative types proceed, we shall confine ourselves to pointing once again to their connections with the achievements of children in the fields of pictorial and plastic art, because the basic experiences underlying their work also do not spring from sight. That is why expressive overemphases are found in the drawings of children as much as in those of the weak sighted and in the modelling of the blind.

(4) *The Symbolic Representation of Space and Time*

While instructing the blind in the art of modelling I frequently observed that they translated into rhythmical forms rhythm occurring in a temporal sequence. Thus one congenitally blind pupil indicated a heart beating with excitement by rhythmical ridges between the ribs. Another one showed that the mouth was trembling by carving the lips in an undulating shape. A third (Pl. 76) treated the trembling or blinking of the eyes in a similar fashion. From this, it appears that in the art of the blind, space and time are often fused into a unity.

We find exactly the same characteristics in the representations of the haptic type of weak sighted. H. A. portrayed a man who had been frightened (Pl. 23), by surrounding the lips with wavy lines and similar wavy lines are to be found around the chin. When I asked what was the meaning of this symbol H. A. answered " His chin too is trembling ".

This example shows that the haptic type, whether he be weak sighted or blind, succeeds in solving the problem of the difference between space and time sequences. The expressive strength of his subjective experiences transcends the dualism and makes possible the harmonious symbolisation of the artistic expression of experience.

(5) *Summary*

The comparative study of the pictorial work of the weak sighted and the plastic work of the blind shows :

(i) That the total impression of unity in both cases has been achieved by a constructive synthesis of partial impressions.

(ii) That a conception of the work as a whole is present *a priori* only when the subjective determination of experiences is dominant.

(iii) When autoplastic experience becomes the basis of creative work, the relative sizes and proportions of objects drawn or modelled by the weak sighted and the blind are determined by value judgments and by their emotional significance for the artist.

(iv) The haptic type does not integrate its symbols of form and expression in a way that normal sighted people would regard as ' naturalistic '.

(v) The *visual* weak sighted type is capable of developing to the point at which he represents light and shade in a manner corresponding to ' normal ' vision, just as the *visual* type of blind artist achieves a ' naturalistic ' composition.

(vi) Weak sighted and blind haptic types translate rhythms of movement and sound into form rhythms. In other words space and time are fused into a unity in their compositions.

(vii) The procedure of the weak sighted approximates very closely indeed to that of the blind and in both cases the fundamental creative types find the forms of expression that are adequate to their type.

(*e*) THE POSSIBILITY OF DEVELOPING FROM HAPTIC PERCEPTION
TO VISUAL IMAGING

After what has been said, we cannot without qualification admit that it is possible to develop from the haptic mode of perception to the attainment of a visual image. We have seen that there are two fundamentally different types, two *Weltanschauungen*. The one is at home in the world of visual appearances, the other starts more from haptic experiences and emphasises his subjective life. It must be remembered that ' haptic experience ' has been defined somewhat more broadly than is usual. We have now to determine whether one type can develop into the other so completely that when his attitude to form and shape has been changed his whole mental attitude is also changed, for unless this is so one cannot speak of development in any real sense.

' Development ' is usually understood as being a development from the inferior to the superior, from poorer quality to better. I shall not use the word in this sense. A superficial review might lead one to believe that the haptic type is the inferior one. His work is, as we shall see, closely related to the creative art of primitive peoples and to certain trends which are found in modern art all over the world, especially in the expressionist school. A lower rating of the haptic type would be completely false, for the mental level at which a type works depends only on the kind and intensity of his spiritual conception and on the quality of his intellect. There are highly developed haptic forms of art just as there are highly developed visual forms of art. Each form will receive its clearest expression through an artist of the pure haptic or pure visual type. But in most cases visual and haptic influences make themselves felt simultaneously, *although there is usually a preference for the one or the other type of experience*[1]. We may be able to speak of a development from one type to the other only if visual perception as well as haptic experiences of form become integral parts of artistic experience.

M. B. and Sch. G. at first worked apparently solely with haptic impressions, that is, their representative symbols of form and expression were autoplastic and determined entirely by their bodily sensations (Pls. 5, 41, 42). The origin as well as the final appearance of their work was devoid of visual influences. Only when they had been made to draw did they become aware of their visual surroundings and begin to take an interest in them, so that new elements of shape came within their powers. Although M. B. confined herself almost entirely to figures and heads, the way in which these were drawn gradually underwent a change. The individual representatives of shape and expression changed. The symbols for the eye sockets, which appeared as darker ovals, gradually lost their original significance. To begin with they symbolised the basis for the eyes which as before were drawn as discs with darker circles in the middle (eyes and pupils) over which the lids were added later. Gradually

---

[1] Lowenfeld, Viktor, *Tests for Visual and Haptical Aptitudes*, American Journal of Psychology, Vol. 58, No. 1, 1945, pp. 100-11.

they began to lose the meaning of hollows and took on the surface character of shadows around the deep set eyes. In Pls. 43–46 we can trace quite clearly the gradual changes and the development of this form symbol from hollow to shadow. The nose, which to begin with had been 'added' as an independent form symbol in a darker colour or even constructed separately by means of a circumscribing line, began to be recognized visually as a projecting part. Consequently the line separating it from the rest of the face changed in meaning. The lines surrounding the nose were at first symmetrical on the left and the right, but later they became stronger on one side, until, in Pl. 44, we see that the burning candle throws a shadow. The same development is undergone by the darker shade that symbolises 'taking away' the cheek. This, too, begins to indicate a shadow.

To begin with, the individual representatives of form and expression symbolised sometimes a hollow and at other times an addition or subtraction of forms. At this stage, however, they attain an increasing *visual* significance. They begin to be more and more co-ordinated in a picture the aspect of which is related to that derived from visual perception although this was not its original starting point. At the same time we can see how the individual symbols, which in Pl. 41 are still completely isolated, are more and more subordinated to the picture as a whole. The picture takes on a progressively more naturalistic character typical of visual compositions.

A further essential factor that now enters M. B.'s work is a spontaneous change in technique. She chooses one that most clearly shows up the importance of light and shade. She denies herself colour effects and concentrates on the tones of light and dark (Pl. 15). In addition we should observe the extremely interesting fact that through the tremendous change in her will to pictorial expression, which leads her work into its natural line of development, her drawing has to start anew and in a series of jumps recapitulates its ontogenetic development up to its final level of achievement. Pl. 45 again shows that apparently naturalistic style of drawing in which, as Münz says, the individual representative symbols have not been thoroughly articulated, and the conception of the whole remains diffuse. The wrinkles on the forehead are only superficially indicated. The nose has been portrayed only roughly. The individual vehicles of expression are undifferentiated and drawn rather uncertainly. It is a rather undifferentiated representation of the total impression of a face. In the next drawing (Pl. 46) we find the same stage of development which we have already discussed in the developmental series of H. A. in Pl. 19. We have here the same apparently constructional style in which the individual symbols seem to have become petrefacts, crystallised too sharply through the process of coming to consciousness. It is this process that induces M. B. in contrast to her last coloured attempts to surround the symbol for nose in the same way as H. A. did in his drawing in Pl. 19. The eyebrows and eyes, too, are connected with the nose in that strongly symmetrical manner we have found to be characteristic of this stage of development. The symmetrical lines of tension running down from the nose, which represent an autoplastic experience and therefore include the chin, and the uniform unrealistic stringing together of the teeth, are also characteristic and similar to Pls. 19 and 5b. Indeed the parallelism of these drawings is startling and can only be explained by the circumstance that M. B., faced with this new problem of representing shape, has had to start again at the very beginning. Gradually, however, this inflexibility begins to dissolve (Pl. 47). The unrelieved symmetry begins to diminish. The individual representative symbols begin to come alive and fill the face with expression. The unvaried line circumscribing the nose begins to develop signs of being used to represent light and shade, as may be seen from the strengthening of one of the lines. If we compare the lines running away from the nostrils with the ones in the previous picture, we see that they are becoming much looser. The teeth, too, have lost the character of simply being strung together. Even at this stage of development we can clearly see the tendency towards the representation of visual form. The characteristic developmental series of the haptic type, for example Pl. 16 by H. A., shows that the individual representative symbols whilst remaining completely separate from each other, are more and more differentiated and articulated. Pl. 15, however, shows that what is characteristic of the visual type is that these individual representatives are increasingly subordinated to the total picture within which light and shade begin to play an increasing part. Pl. 48 shows this process even more clearly. Here not only the shading of objects but also the shadows thrown by objects begin to be indicated. In Pl. 49 visual appearances and the play of light and shade dominate the picture. Merely symbolic representatives of expression have almost entirely disappeared. It is the visual aspect of the nose which is portrayed, without any bounding line. More and more we see how visual appearances are co-ordinated to create the impression of a visual whole. Though this picture is not a final product, the end to which it is tending is becoming clearly visible. Sch. G., on the other hand, after he had completed Pl. 50, " Beggar," in which for the first time he had attempted to solve the problems of space by means of shadows, that is optically, turned away from the representation of figures. Though a naturalistic picture has not yet been achieved—the individual symbols of form and expression in the faces are still treated in isolation and are individually recognizable as such—the way in which shadows are drawn clearly indicates the visual impulse. From now on the figure becomes for him no more than a subsidiary object within a wider spatial setting, the problems of which absorb his whole attention.

Here, too, we can follow exactly the development from the haptic to the visual articulation of space. In his earlier drawings (cf. Pl. 38) space is still closely related to his individual experience and the relationship between figure and space is determined by value judgments. Gradually, however, Sch. G. proceeded to a more ' objective ' representation of space. His first drawings were done in a bird's-eye view manner, which enabled him to make a transition from " feeling his way " in space to visual representation (Pl. 33). Later his drawings developed a more uniform aspect distinguished by a more ' correct ' perception of size and proportion. Pl. 40 is one of a series of houses drawn as seen from in front. As may be seen from Pl. 37, the inner necessity to combine his need for orientation in space with this particular manner of drawing led him to a form of drawing that approximates closely to naturalistic representation. He here attempted to fuse the knowledge of size and proportion, which he had gained through drawing frontal aspects, with his knowledge of depth, which he had tried to incorporate in the bird's-eye view. In the development of his drawings, through which he became aware that objects at a distance appear smaller so that he actually began to draw perspectivally, his high intelligence must probably be regarded as an important factor, though his visual attitude to his environment is his primary characteristic and shows itself in many different ways. Pl. 51 is an exceedingly naturalistic drawing that has been built up logically and constructively just like Pl. 33, which has already been discussed. Here, too, Sch. G. started from a kind of ' plan ' by means of which he orientated himself in space. He began first with the background and gradually completed the drawing towards the foreground. A closer inspection shows that the church was at first completed, only to be hidden by trees later.

In the two typical cases discussed above we have seen an undoubted development from haptic to visual representation. The question arises whether we are also entitled to say that a change of creative *type* has taken place. This is not so, for in both cases all we were able to show was that the pupils were able to remove inhibitions and disabilities standing in the way of the full unfolding of their most fundamental creative impulses. If the basic talent had not been visual, neither of the two cases would have been able to achieve a type of drawing conforming to normal visual impressions. The development in both cases merely shows that the beginnings of creative activities by means of drawings appear to be the same and that those whose talent is visual also pass through the haptic developmental stage. In other words, a development from haptic perception to visual imagination takes place only when a talent for visual drawing is *a priori* present. The particular consciousness of form and the mode of representation are deeply rooted psychological characteristics, which seem to disappear only when the personality ceases to exist.

CHAPTER VII

THE RELATION OF SUBJECTIVATING AND OBJECTIVATING ATTITUDES IN ART

The systematic study of art has always been concerned with the fact that in the development of art forms two aims and two styles seem to be traceable. Throughout the whole history of art these two styles and two contrary impulses have stood in opposition. Some have spoken of geometric and naturalistic art. Schiller contraster the ' naïve ' and the ' sentimental ' styles. Nietzsche spoke of ' apollonian ' and ' dionysian ' and attempted thereby to characterise two conceptions of art which arise from different ways of representing the relations between things the formal aspects of which have presented the artist with pictorial problems. Not until fairly recently were attempts made to analyse these contrary impulses more deeply. Alois Riegl in particular endeavoured to understand the nature of these art styles instead of subjecting them merely to aesthetic judgments.[1] He thought very deeply about the nature of ' geometrical ' style and contrasted it with the ' naturalistic '. Verworn speaks of ' ideoplastic ' and ' physioplastic ' art.[2] By physioplastic art he understands compositions " consisting of a direct reproduction of the natural object or of its immediate memory image ". He uses the term ideoplastic art when the representations do not spring from immediate observation but express ideas, deductions or abstract knowledge. Danzel contrasts ' static ' and ' dynamic ' types of art.[3] By this rather vague formulation he intends to express his view that for the static type of artist the tendency to strictness and systematization predominates, whilst the dynamic

[1] Alois Riegl, *Stilfragen*. Berlin, 1923.
[2] Max Verworn, *Ideoplastische Kunst*. Jena, 1914.
[3] Theodor Wilhelm Danzel, *Kultur und Religionen des Primitiven Menschen.* Stuttgart, 1924.

type of artist is concerned " with somehow expressing and bearing witness to the life that flows through him ". That is, " he attempts to express individual experiences." Herbert Kühn was of the opinion that the nature of these stylistic opposites could be most clearly formulated by the words ' sensorial ' and ' imaginative '.[1] By sensorial he understands those art forms which most strongly express the fact that the artist is concerned through his senses with what goes on around him, whilst the concept of the imaginative style applies to those who stand apart from life, who consciously turn away from nature to the things that lie beyond. The form of expression of sensorial art, he says, is the copy of reality, the imitation of nature, the reproduction of objects and their bounding lines, the representation of fleeting aspects, of change itself. Imaginative art, on the other hand, attempts to hold on to what is permanent and universal in objects, to that which expresses their inner unity and nature and the laws of their existence.

All these views have one thing in common : what is visually perceptible in the external universe is contrasted with what is seen with the ' inward senses ', with what is experienced. Art consists in depicting the relations of the artist to the world of his experiences, that is, in depicting his experience with objects and not the objects themselves. In other words, what is of final importance is the *manner* of experience which decisively determines the products of the artist. If we look at it in this way we can understand that in the art of the weak sighted, on the frontiers between sight and blindness, we find artistic types whose creations may be sensorial and imaginative, physioplastic or ideoplastic at the same time. This will depend on the artist's attitude to the creative processes, whether it was determined by what is sensorially perceptible or by the tendency to blindness, which implies standing apart from what is given in nature and seeking to portray only " what is permanent and universal in objects, what expresses their inner unity and nature and the laws of their existence ". But the existence of the two creative types whose pure forms we have

---

[1] Herbert Kühn, *Die Kunst der Primitiven.* Munich, 1923.

so far discussed in this book urgently demands that they should be related to the two main currents of style in art. In what has gone before we attempted to elucidate the relationship of the two weak sighted creative types to objects and to problems of space, and this investigation will enable us to show that far reaching parallels are to be found in other spheres of art.   In this way we shall find new ways of approaching the problems of the development of style in art.

(a) THE ART OF CHILDREN AND PRIMITIVE ART

As soon as people started to concern themselves with the art of children they realised that parallel phenomena were to be found in the works of primitive races.   As early as 1887 C. Ricci pointed this out and since that time numerous writers have drawn attention to these phenomena, but only very few have attempted to reduce them to systematic order so that deductions could be drawn about the underlying creative impulses.   Verworn in his book on ideoplastic art has gone further than anyone else in attempting to under-stand the meaning of this parallelism.   Our investigations have shown that work which is comparable to primitive art is to be found in the drawings of children only in those cases in which visual experiences are not an integral part of the creative impulses, in other words, where the work of art neither mediately nor immediately arises out of the observation of nature.

It is no wonder, therefore, that in the art of weak sighted children we find in their purest form all those parallels to primitive art that otherwise are to be found only in occasional examples.   Our next problem is to consider how far this kind of analyses of the drawings of weak sighted children and their psychological roots can be applied to the works of primitive peoples.

To begin with it must be observed that it is not feasible to compare, as has so often been done, the work of adults with the work of children.   Adults not only have complete control over their bodies but are frequently highly sophisti-cated in technical matters.   It is important to take into account developmental differences such as these. Neverthe-less, a highly developed Assyrian work of art, for example, may originate in the same conception of space peculiar to the drawing of an undeveloped child.

Bearing these considerations in mind I shall attempt to display and to delimit the main fields in which parallel phenomena can be demonstrated, in the hope that this may make it easier for us to uncover the impulses common to them. I shall bring forward only a few examples and shall leave it to the reader to carry out a systematic survey on the basis of my work on weak sighted children.

The fact that in the art of weak sighted children there is no representation of visual experiences but a translation of thought processes in which haptic perception plays an essential part, excludes from the very beginning any com-parison with works of art in which visual experience plays an integrating rôle. Consequently we shall search as fruitlessly for parallels to the art of children among palæo-lithic works of art as among modern impressionistic paintings. The art of children is throughout ideoplastic or imaginative and we shall therefore have to confine our search to works of art the essence of which is imaginative. But, as we shall see, even in imaginative art there are creative principles that go beyond the intellectual capacity of the child and therefore lie beyond his creative impulses. Let us, therefore, begin by asking what kinds of art must contain components that are also to be found in the art of children. We shall have to ignore the scribbling stage because, as Krötzsch has shown, it is an expression of rhythmical impulses belonging to a time before a causal connection can be deliberately estab-lished between the impulse to movement and the line that follows. These impulsive expressions that gradually lead to stages in which there is a more or less conscious attempt to direct lines, are specifically childish beginnings and can only be compared to other childish beginnings. We are concerned specifically with conscious expressions, even though they may take very primitive forms.

The early developmental stages of child art show that a certain relationship with objects has been established. If

we take this object relation as a consistent type of representation, we have to exclude from our considerations drawings
the object of which is mere ornamentation.   My analyses
of the drawings of weak sighted children have shown that,
however symbolical they may be, they always reflect the
relation of the picture to some image.   That is, ornamentation even in its early play aspects is completely lacking.
The reason for this is probably that the child is always
concerned with *communicating* something.   Where ornamentation appears in the art of primitive peoples as an expressive
principle we find that the child chooses other means to
symbolise the same expressive intention :   the impressive
decorations of a chief or a god would be expressed by means
of overemphasising relative proportions.   The rich ornamentation of Mexican or African cultures finds no parallel in the
art of children.   Again, in the drawings of the weak sighted
we find no tendency to symmetry, though in the art of
primitive peoples this symbolises the eternal, the absolute,
the religious.   The child, bound as it is to its individual
experience, recreates in pictorial form its own individual
experience.   But in doing so it also uses signs to symbolise
values, and in this way generalises its individual modes of
expression.   Therefore, the practical or utilitarian must also
be excluded from our comparative study.

It is now clear that the real field of primitive art with which
we have to make comparisons is that in which the creative
impulses are determined by subjective relationships to
reality.   In this field we find the most far reaching parallelism
both in the representation of space and in the manner by
which expressions are symbolised by means of shapes.   We
find overemphasis employed to symbolise the importance
or significance of that which is represented as well as overemphases determined by bodily experiences.   We find that
in representing space, the base line is used in exactly the same
way as it is in the drawings of the weak sighted.   The same
laws explain the interpenetration of plan and elevation,
which are utilised as principles in drawings whenever they
are connected by some representational intention.   Similarly
we find subjective or affectively toned space, in fact all the

components of a composition that we have been able to isolate in the art of weak sighted children. Further, we have found that the haptic creative type represents one form of the more mature development of artistic characteristics of the work of the weak sighted and in the following chapters I shall attempt to show that the art forms of this creative type are common among primitive peoples. But first I shall examine briefly the naturalistic representation of palæolithic cave dwellers, a discussion of which also arises out of the analysis of the art of the weak sighted.

(b) PHENOMENOLOGICAL OBSERVATIONS ON THE NATURALISTIC REPRESENTATIONS OF THE MOST PRIMITIVE PEOPLES

Attempts are repeatedly made to deduce the development of art as a whole from the development of the art of children. We know now that when a child begins consciously to concern itself with artistic productions, that is, when it has developed sufficient control over its muscles to be able to establish deliberately a relation between the picture and that which it depicts, its representations are by no means modelled on nature ; they tend to be symbolic, as my work and that of many others has shown. That is, children introduce signs having only an indirect relation to the things represented. At this point the consciousness of the child is already filled with thoughts and feelings and these naturally are expressed in their drawings. Verworn rightly observes that all European children produce drawings which are perfect examples of ideoplastic art and paradigmatically illuminate the psychology of ideoplastic processes. But we also know that at the earliest beginnings of artistic production in prehistoric times, there existed an art form the creative impulses of which were directed solely by attempts to copy nature. This is the art of the palæolithic hunter. These compositions, which Verworn quotes as pure examples of physioplastic art, stand in the strongest possible contradiction to the fundamental biogenetic law according to which ontogenesis—by which we would mean in this connection the development of the art of children—is a condensed recapitulation of phylogenesis—by which we would here mean the development of art as a whole. This fact led Verworn to conclude that there is not the remotest possibility of establishing a parallelism between the development of the art of children and prehistoric art in the sense of the biogenetic law. This conclusion can certainly not be questioned if we inspect the available material of children's drawings, although Verworn maintains that the ideoplastic art of the child represents a higher level of mental activity than the naïve physioplastic art of earlier times. In the art of children there does not seem to be a physioplastic stage preceding the ideoplastic stage. Apparently, then, Verworn is right ; but not for the reason which he gives. He maintains that the reason lies in the fact of education, that is, that the consciousness of the child is filled with all sorts of ideas before it proceeds to attempt to represent objects. The reason lies not in education, however, but in the inability to control its muscles accurately enough before it reaches the ideoplastic level. Bühler, therefore, raises the question whether it is feasible to assume that at a very early age the child potentially possesses the capacity of reproducing naïve physioplastic drawings and whether it would do so if it had sufficient control over its musculature.[1]   We know that long before the child begins to draw it is perfectly capable not only of perceiving but also of understanding differences between objects. I shall attempt to answer Bühler's question by means of my investigations.

In the developed drawings of the weak sighted we possess documents, that like the models of the blind, were begun after the infantile stage had been passed. The developmental series by H. A. and M. B. (Pls. 15 and 16) may serve as a basis for our discussion. Both artists set to work without any previous training.   Like very young children they had to start their creative processes at the very beginning. There is therefore far more justification for comparing their work with that of primitive peoples, as we are no longer faced with the great discrepancy between child and adult. We are comparing two sets of people who are fully able to use

[1] Karl Bühler, *The Mental Development of the Child.* London, 1931.

their available senses. Now both my investigations of the drawings of the weak sighted as well as those of Ludwig Münz of the plastic work of the blind, show that the first stage of artistic work is naturalistic. Münz named it the ' pseudo naturalistic stage ' and compared it with the apparently naturalistic drawings of people with normal vision at the distant beginning of human artistic endeavour. But he believed that those early shapes already contain individualised symbols and appear naturalistic only because the individual symbols have not as yet been thoroughly articulated and because their perception is as yet diffuse and necessarily generalised. This may be true of the formative efforts of the blind, but I believe he is mistaken when he thinks the same is true of prehistoric art. Prehistoric art may perhaps be regarded as being at a level which is still below that attained by the blind and the weak sighted because of the superior development of their intellect. But from the psychological point of view this first stage in the work of the blind and the weak sighted is exactly equivalent to the physioplastic art forms discussed by Verworn in connection with palæolithic art. There is as yet no synthesis of individually observed things. The object has been perceived as a whole in a way that is similar to the ' photogramme ' of the daily visual impressions made on the palæolithic hunter by his prey. If we look at the two developmental series of Pls. 15 and 16 we see that contents of thought and feeling are more and more introduced into the drawings and are frequently symbolised quite abstractly. At the end of the series we are no longer dealing with the total impression made upon the senses, but with pure ideoplastic art the synthetic principles of which are clearly apparent.

Thus we see that ontogenetically the first work of the weak sighted and the blind obeys the biogenetic law. We are therefore probably justified in affirming the hypothesis that the art of normal children misses out the first stages of artistic development only because of the lack of muscular control. We find the stage corresponding to that of prehistoric man in the work of the weak sighted and the blind because of their greater muscular and intellectual development as a result of which they are ontogenetically capable of recapitulating the artistic history of the race.[1]

(c) HAPTIC SPACE IN ART

We shall find spatial compositions that remind us of the compositions of the weak sighted, only in cases in which impressions are represented that directly or indirectly spring from *subjective* feeling about space or bodily sensations. We must, however, exercise care in the interpretation of this generalization. In the art of children it is only the *first* experience of space that springs from a subjective relation to the environment. Repetition makes it habitual and it becomes a generalised schema just as in all art the originally subjective experience becomes through tradition a generally accepted style. Only in these terms can we understand, for example, the significance of the base line in Egyptian art which, originating in the subjective experience of things standing on or growing vertically from a basis, is gradually given its symbolic meaning both as basis and as boundary, as plane and as space at the same time. In the drawings of the weak sighted we were able to follow the various individual phases of this mode of representing space. It appears in the same way in Australian drawings made on the bark of trees, the drawings of Indians and those of Arctic tribes. The same method of treating space is to be found in manuscripts and miniatures of the Middle Ages. But the most perfect examples of the development of haptic space are to be found in Babylonian, Assyrian and Egyptian art.[1]

The scope of this book does not permit me to do more than display some characteristic examples. These, though systematic, are by no means exhaustive and are intended merely to indicate parallel laws of composition in different works of art.

Pls. 53 *a* and *b* and Pl. 60 all show in exactly the same way that the base line is considered merely as a support for the trees which stand on it. We see how the trees grow upwards

[1] Lowenfeld, V., *Psycho-Aesthetic Implications of the Art of the Blind*, The Journal of Aesthetics and Art Criticism, Vol. X, No. 1, 1951.

from one base line only as far as the next one, which is also the boundary line for the water. The plane on which they stand is level and its symbol, the base line, is therefore straight. When the terrain changes, as in the hilly deserts of Egypt, the base line also changes and by its curves and irregularities fits the nature of the terrain.[1] A comparison of figs. 48 and 49 and Pl. 61 will make this clear. The Assyrian picture of Pl. 62 is a particularly fine example of the way in which objects are related to their base line. In the background we see an almost exact replica of the weak sighted drawing in fig. 43. On a plain—the lowest straight base line—there are mountains symbolised by new wavy base lines. On the mountains there are trees. Here the outline of the hills is also the base line of the trees, which grow vertically away from it, just as in the drawings of weak sighted pupils. In the right foreground there is a hill up which workers are carrying their burdens. This may now be compared with figs. 45 and 46. It seems to me quite likely that the warriors are thought to be standing on top of the hill, which explains why the horizontal base line on which they stand has been brought into contact with the top of the hill, exactly as in fig. 45. So much for the representation of 'objective space'.

Pl. 63a,[2] makes a transition from objective space to subjective or affectively toned space. It is an Egyptian drawing of a garden with a pond out of which water carriers are fetching water. Clearly an attempt has been made to show that the trees grow 'upwards' from the base lines; it would be wrong to say that they had been 'folded over'. It is to be particularly noted, however, that it is only the water which appears in plan; everything else, trees, lotus blossoms, water carriers and pitchers has been drawn in elevation. This alternation in the two spatial aspects is to be explained by reference to subjective attitudes towards the various objects depicted. The water is surrounded by trees and reeds. If, then, we wish to appreciate the pond as a four sided object,

---

[1] This has been systematically demonstrated by Heinrich Schäfer in his book *Von Agyptischer Kunst, besonders der Zeichenkunst*, Leipzig, 1919, from which Pl. 61 has been reproduced.

[2] Pls. 63 a and b have both been taken from Schäfer.

it has to be drawn in plan. Lotus flowers, however, do not show their characteristics if they are drawn from above. In the same way the pitchers and the figures have been drawn ' orthoscopically ' because their most important characteristics are also best seen in side elevation. These subjective factors in the treatment of space can be seen even more clearly in Pl. 63*b* which represents a basket and its contents. The tray on which the basket stands is drawn in side elevation, whilst the basket and its contents have been drawn in plan, a clear indication that the intention was to portray the contents (cf. figs. 51, 58, and 60). Of very great interest is the comparison of the drawings of steps in Pls. 64 *a* and *b* and in figs. 46 and 50. Pl. 64*b* depicts saying farewell to a mummy at the tomb. The shaft *down* which the guardian of souls in the shape of a bird brings food and drink has also been drawn. The steps going downwards are indicated by means of *parallel* lines, just as in the weak sighted drawing of fig. 50, whilst the steps going upwards to the throne of the king (Pl. 64*a*), are represented orthoscopically by a broken line again exactly as in the weak sighted drawing. Incidentally we may notice that Pl. 64*b* is one of those numerous ' X-ray drawings ' which we know so well from the drawings of children. To these few yet characteristic examples we could add many others from other times and other art styles. I am, however, only concerned with pointing out parallel phenomena for we have already carried out a thorough phenomenological investigation in the case of the work of the weak sighted.[1]

The treatment of temporally separated events in one composition also belongs to haptic space. This phenomenon can be seen in primitive art as well as in Egyptian art. Even in works of the late Middle Ages we can trace the strongly expressive subjective factors that lead to the analytic representation of the concepts of space and time. Heinrich

[1] The reader's attention is drawn to the splendid examples of conflicts between plan and front elevation and of ' folding over ' in the *Heidelberg MS.*, to the countless paintings of the Last Supper, in which we find the table drawn in plan and the glasses in elevation, to the Mexican *Codex Mendoza* in which the same treatment is effectively used and to the valuable examples in Heinrich Schäfer's *Von Ägyptischer Kunst*.

Schäfer describes Egyptian pictures of dancers in which the movements of a dancer are separately represented in one picture, as on a modern strip of film. Pl. 64*b* shows us a mummy before it is let down into the tomb and then when it is already lying in the tomb. Ludwig Münz compares the plastic treatment of space and time by the blind with that to be found in primitive art. He quotes Heinz Werner[1] who shows that ' natural man ' does not differentiate between the artistic reproduction of space and of time and illustrates this by means of an Indian drawing in which the flight of a white man has been represented by a wavy line. I myself have seen a Kwakiutl drawing which represents a scene in the ritual of a secret society. In it a dancer castigates himself by inflicting wounds on himself with a knife whilst his companions put heated stones into the wound and pull them out again. In this drawing the placing and withdrawing of the stones is represented by means of a wavy line proceeding from the wound to the stone and back again (in this connection compare, for example, figs. 55 and 56). But this particular phenomenon can be found elsewhere than among ' natural men '. Wickhoff[2] discusses the phenomenon at great length in connection with the Vienna *Genesis*. Also in the miniatures of books on German law (*Sachsenspiegel*) we see figures with gesticulating hands. Frequently their characteristic movement has been represented by means of two pairs of hands (Pl. 65).

If we compare the treatment of haptic space in works of art of many different kinds and origins and in the drawings of the weak sighted, we find a very far reaching correspondence. This correspondence occurs wherever the haptic creative type expresses through works of art its subjective relation to its environment.

(*d*) EXPRESSIVE OVEREMPHASIS AND THE AUTOPLASTIC EXPERIENCE OF FORM

The analysis of the creative work of the weak sighted reveals two other characteristics, the overemphasis of

---

[1] Heinz Werner, *Raum und Zeit in den Urformen der Künste.*
[2] Wickhoff and Härtel, *Die Wiener Genesis.* Compare also the Manessian MS.

important things and the representation of bodily experiences. These two factors are characteristic of the same creative type the expressions of which we have hitherto followed in the art of various peoples and epochs. A consideration of all these various phenomena seems to me to make it quite certain that they are all expressions of the same creative type, which we have called the haptic type. We can also see that certain cultural epochs and levels have their parallels in the developmental stages in the art of the weak sighted and the blind. The first developmental stage has, with certain reservations, been compared to the earliest beginnings of art in palæolithic times (Pls. 15 and 16). In discussing the relationship of the art of children to primitive art, we have seen that symmetry, and the whole decorative and ornamental impulses it marks, is not to be found among the artistic impulses of the child. But the developmental series represented in Pls. 15 and 16 show that the second stage in the development of drawings necessarily leads to symmetrical composition.

At this developmental stage there is a strong impulse to constructional drawing and I have connected this with the fact that the artist suddenly becomes conscious of his autoplastic experiences and that this powerful realisation of the nature of bodily experience leads to an exaggerated emphasis of the individual forms indicating expression. But this realisation that there are regular relations between particular sensations and their external manifestation as expression, also leads to an overemphasis of common factors or laws. In other words, it leads to symmetry, which is an expression of the artist's realisation that there are valid absolutes and eternal verities. Out of the chaos of indeterminate shapes (cf. the first stages, Nos. 1 and 2 in Pl. 16) appears order, or what Herbert Kühn has called " the eternal unity and the essence of things ".[1] Can we not say that here symmetry has achieved its truest significance ? When we investigate the way in which this symmetry manifests itself, we shall find in most of the drawings of the weak sighted and of primitive peoples that representative

[1] Herbert Kühn, *Die Kunst der Primitiven*.

symbols which at first are merely indicated vaguely are later displayed by means of firm lines (Pl. 16, 3). Indicators of expression and parts of the face that are related to one another or occur on both sides are circumscribed by a line or lines (Pl. 66). The eyebrows, combined with the nose and frequently also with the eyes, readily lend themselves to ornamental treatment. The folds going downwards from the nose are often fused with the chin to form a symmetrical structure which includes the mouth. Thus in the ancestral mask from New Mecklenburg (Pl. 66) the eyebrows and the chin have been symmetrically included and this framing of eyes and mouth considerably heightens the dæmonic impression. In Pl. 67, on the other hand, a mask from New Guinea, the eyebrows and the nose form a symmetrical structure (cf. with this Pl. 47). Where facial expressions originating from feelings of muscular innervation are repeated, forms arise which, because of the number of parallel lines, give the impression of being almost pure ornaments. Pls. 68 and 69 are instructive. The latter is from Pacasmayo in Peru, the former was done in one of my classes by T. H. who has been blind since birth. The only difference is that in his mask the individual lineaments have been more highly individuated. Mexican art is full of examples of this autoplastic type of sculpture, in which we can see very clearly that the auto- plastically drawn lineaments do not correspond to visual experiences and are of the same type as that discussed by Ludwig Münz in connection with the plastic work of the blind (Pl. 70). The way in which the nose is pulled together does not correspond to a visual impression, but is expressed by lines which result from the muscular sensations around the nose. The developmental series of Pl. 16 shows that as the intensity of individual experience grows, the inflexibility of symmetrical representation begins to disappear.[1] It should be remembered, of course, that the liberation from inflexible symmetry does not necessarily mean that a better work of art is produced. For example, the expressive mask

[1] The same was shown by L. Münz to be true of the figures modelled by my blind pupils.

" Listener " by G. St. (Pl. 30) is certainly at a lower artistic level than the masks by H. A. (Pl. 16) although the former is much more asymmetric than the latter. Pl. 71 and Pl. 30 can be compared in the same way. The Singhalese mask shows clearly that the one-sided distortion of the face has also affected the nose, and that corresponds to autoplastic experience. The strong tension on the cheeks has affected not only the mouth, but, exactly as in the weak sighted mask of Pl. 30, the teeth as well which, since they are part of the skeleton, are visually not affected. Here then we again have work by the same types that we discussed in previous chapters.

Again, exactly as in the case of the weak sighted or the blind, we see that overemphases can have two meanings. They express the importance which the emphasised parts assume within the composition as a whole, or they express autoplastic bodily experiences. Pl. 72 shows a figure from New Mecklenburg which represents a man listening. Both his ears and his hands have been overemphasised because both are important for catching the sound. Verworn describes amulets which are exaggerated in similar directions.[1] In eastern Siberia a carved wooden amulet is used to protect the wearer against stiffness in the joints of the arm. The amulets represent a human figure but consist only of a small head and a very large arm containing movable joints. The arm with its movable joints is the important thing. The head is necessary merely to indicate that the representation is that of the human body ; everything else has been omitted because it is inessential. The " Orator " of Pl. 55 shows the same principles at work. The audience is depicted by a number of heads and arms and everything else has been omitted. The arms are important because they hold the waving handkerchiefs of the crowd which is cheering the speaker ; the heads indicate merely that we are dealing with human beings. The illustration from the *Egbert Codex* (Pl. 73), dating from the Middle Ages, is one of many examples with similar pictorial principles. Fig. 19 shows " a Man Yawning ". The most important expressive symbol

[1] Verworn, *op. cit.*, p. 24.

is the wide open mouth and everything else has been omitted as unimportant. A similar omission of certain parts or the emphasis of others can be found in the masks and drawings of primitive peoples, for example Pl. 74. All these omissions of unimportant and exaggerations of important parts arise out of the impulse to regard the world through the spectacles of value judgments and to assign sizes subjectively, according to the degree of importance attached to one's own individual experience. These " proportions of significance " are to be found throughout the whole range of art wherever artistic expression is not directly determined by visual experience. In Egyptian murals the kings and other prominent persons are made larger in exactly the same way as in Byzantine paintings. Compare, for instance, Pls. 34 and 75. In these cases large and small cannot be regarded as visual qualities : they are expressive valuations ; visual experiences have to make way for impulses lying outside the visual sphere. Works in what has been called the imaginative or ideoplastic style are completely dominated by the artist's subjective relationship to his environment. They find their purest parallels in the products of the weak sighted haptic creative types, because not only physical factors but psychological attitudes as well act together to exclude the world of visible appearances from the field of artistic reproduction.

(e) EXPRESSIONISM AND IMPRESSIONISM AS MANIFESTATIONS OF THE TWO CREATIVE TYPES

The investigations with which we have been concerned in this book have shown that the starting point of artistic experience does not necessarily have to be an experience of the sense of sight but can be haptic in origin. We have further proved that the haptic experience of form is not necessarily determined by the physiological fact that sight is lacking, but that its roots extend deep into psychological attitudes. It is the existence of this psychological attitude that enabled us to compare the haptic creative type expressing itself in the art of the weak sighted with parallel phenomena in art as a whole.

We started out to examine a special and perhaps restricted field. It must therefore be emphasised once more that this investigation does not claim to be complete. All that is intended is that certain important problems that arose in the course of our investigation should be formulated and put forward for discussion.

In the history of art there have been as many changes in the views about the nature of the artistic reproduction of experience and of form as there have been changes in the philosophies of the time. Of all these different conceptions I have treated only the problems of visual and haptic perception, because they arose directly out of the preceding investigations of weak sighted types.

We may divide art forms into two large groups—the impressionistic and the expressionistic. Every work of art can be classified somehow in one or other of these groups. If we assign to the impressionistic group all those forms of art whose starting point lies in what is perceived by the external senses, then the expressionistic forms have as their basis subjective attitudes and bodily experiences. The impressionistic world is the world of appearances ; the world of our senses. The world of expressionistic art is the world of expression, of feelings, of subjective processes. If therefore these haptic artistic experiences are to be sought anywhere they can be sought only where the inner states gave the impulse to creative activity and not where external perception was the integrating factor in artistic experiences and processes. Impressionistic art in painting and in sculpture has always been regarded as visual art whilst expressive art, originating from within, places the self in a value relation to its environment. We shall, therefore, find more and more haptic symbols of form and expression, the more creative activity is bound up with the self and the more immediately the self becomes the centre of artistic experience.

Our investigations of works of art according to the type of artist manifesting itself in them, has been concerned with problems of space as well as the problems of shape and form. We have not, however, attempted to erect the investigations into a system either local or chronological. All that was intended was to display the haptic components to be found in works of widely different ages, epochs, and locations, and to relate them in a general way to all artistic endeavour in painting and sculpture.

As has frequently happened before, the study of an extreme case has resulted in the clarification of a certain field. In this case an analysis of the phenomena of shape and form at the physiological frontiers of blindness, demonstrated that it is the psychological attitude which determines to what creative type an artist belongs. The battle of the two impulses towards orientation in the world of appearances could have been nowhere better demonstrated than in this region where, in order to possess a world of his own, man has himself to create its foundations.

INDEX

FIGURES

The first column gives the number of the figure, the second and third columns the age of the pupil in years and months when the drawing was made.

Scribbling Stage

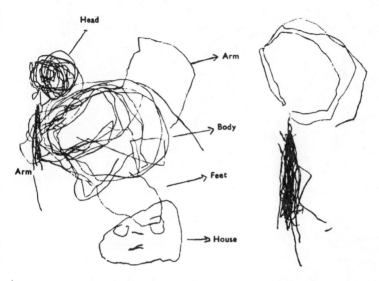

FIG. 1.—9; 9. G. R. First drawing of " Man ". FIG. 2.—9; 10. G. R. First indication of the extension of different parts of the body. Lateral and circular scribbles.

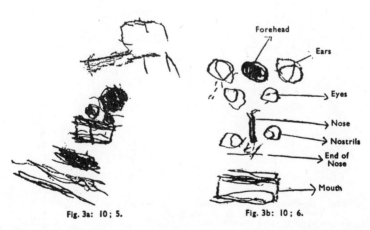

Fig. 3a: 10; 5.

Fig. 3b: 10; 6.

FIG. 3.—Ch. R. Second form of the development of a first human drawing.

155

FIG. 4.—10 ; 8. Ch. R. Pre-
schematic stage. First definite
symbols of expression.

Modifiability of the Schema

FIG. 5.—Normal. " Cannibal."
Special emphasis of mouth
and teeth.

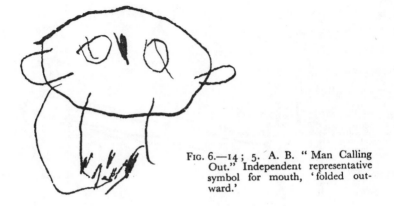

FIG. 6.—14; 5. A. B. "Man Calling Out." Independent representative symbol for mouth, 'folded outward.'

FIG. 7.—9; 5. A. H. "Lifting a Heavy Load." The symbol for "arms" changes.

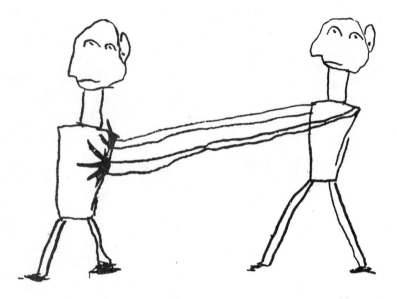

Fig. 8.—11 ; 10. D. H. "Catching." Overemphasis of the catching arm. Omission of unimportant things.

Fig. 9.—8 ; 7. K. W. "Catching." The grasping arm is detached from the body.

FIG. 10.—11 ; 8. D. H. " Normal Representation " of Man (for comparison with Fig. 10a).

FIG. 10a.—11 ; 8. D. H. "A Dog on a Chain is Barking at a Passer-by." The representative symbols for those parts of the body that are particularly intensely experienced have been specially emphasised.

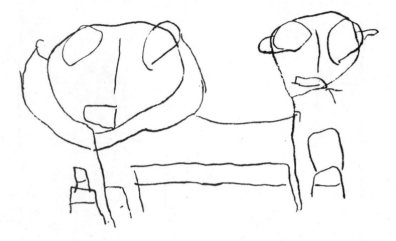

Fig. 11.—10 ; 2. G. R. "Headache." Head enlarged to indicate the experience.

Fig. 12.—11 ; 11. D. H. "Headache." As for Fig. 11.

FIG. 13.—10 ; 6. L. B. Inflexible Schema (for comparison with Fig. 14).

FIG. 14.—10 ; 6. L. B. "Catching." Representation of movement has been transformed into a representation of significances. Running fast indicated by long legs.

Fig. 15.—11 ; 9. D. H. " Man Thinking." Omission of certain representative
symbols for form and expression because of the autoplastic experience of
form. Supporting arm separated from body.

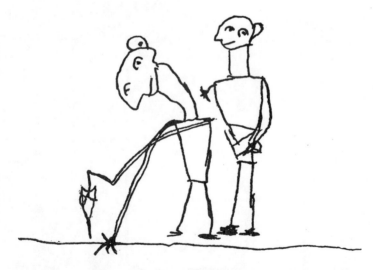

Fig. 16.—11 ; 9. D. H. " Searching for the Lost Pencil." Individual representative symbols emphasised according to the degree of importance of
the bodily experiences.

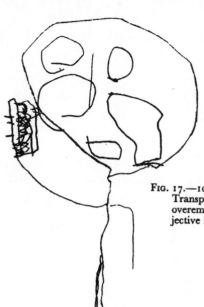

FIG. 17.—10 ; 0. G. R. sees " Her Presents ".
Transposition of individual symbols, and
overemphasis according to degree of subjective importance.

Mimicry and Gesture

FIG. 18.—10 ; 9. Ch. R. " Man
Yawning." First expres-
sive mask

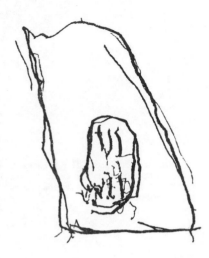

FIG. 19.—9 ; 0. R. F. " Yawning."
Omission of unimportant things.

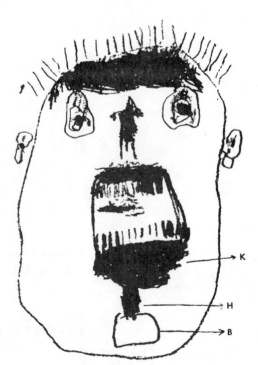

FIG. 20.—9 ; 3. K. W. " Man Yawning." Different symbols of expression are
fused together on the basis of the individual's bodily experience.

FIG. 21.—12 ; 3. D. H. " Man Yawning." Parts of the body that are emphasised and unemphasised receive different treatment.

FIG. 22.—10 ; 2. G. R. " Someone who is Sad."

Fig. 23.—10 ; 4. G. R. "Someone Crying." Separate symbols for tears.

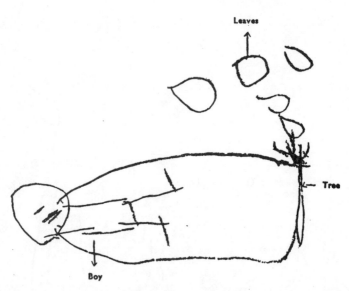

Fig. 24.—13 ; 10. A. B. "Shaking a Nut Tree." Oblique treatment of the figure to indicate the experience.

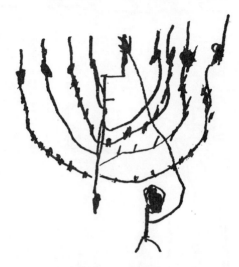

FIG. 25.—8 ; 9. K. W. " Lighting the Candles." Overemphasis of the candle-sticks, which are the centre of interest.

FIG. 26.—11 ; 10. L. B. " Horse Bothered by Flies." Overemphasis of flies.

Fig. 27.—11 ; 9. D. H. "Someone Looking out of a Window."

Fig. 28.—11 ; 8. D. H. "Chess Players." The chess board being of special interest is drawn in plan.

Fig. 29.—8 ; 9. K. W. "K Receives His Birthday Presents." The table bearing the heaviest present is drawn with specially thickened top.

Fig. 30.—8 ; 9. K. W. "A Bad Dog on a Chain." Overemphasis of the chain so that the dog cannot escape.

The Representation of Space

(a) Objective Space

Fig. 31.—11 ; 6. L. B. " Street," single line. Importance of the base line.

Fig. 32.—11 ; 7. L. B. " Street," two lines to indicate the two sides of the street.

FIG. 33.—11 ; 6. L. B. " Street."

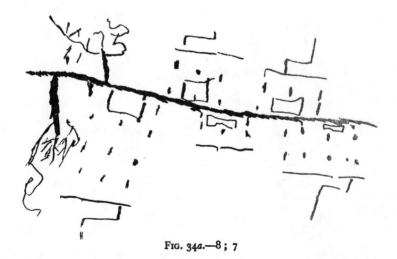

FIG. 34a.—8 ; 7

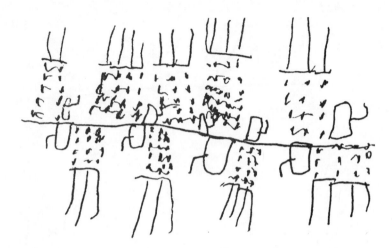

FIG. 34b.—9 ; I. K. W. "Street." Representation of the two sides of a street by 'folding over' away from a single base line.

FIG. 34c.—8 ; 7. K. W. "Street." Subjective experiences demand a drawing with two base lines.

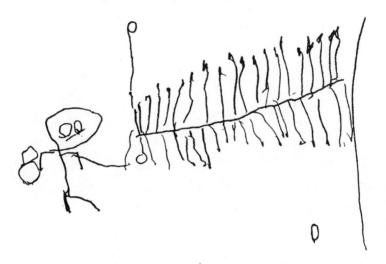

FIG. 35.—10. G. R. "A Girl Picking Flowers." The grass has been 'folded over' to both sides.

(b) *Directions in Space*

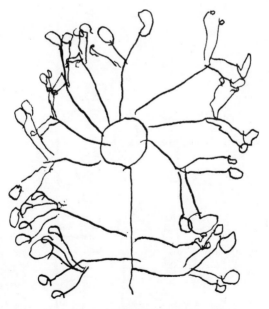

FIG. 36.—9; 10. G. R. Street with Circular Square.

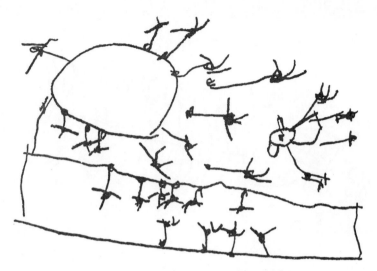

FIG. 37.—13 ; 9. A. B. Street with Circular Square.

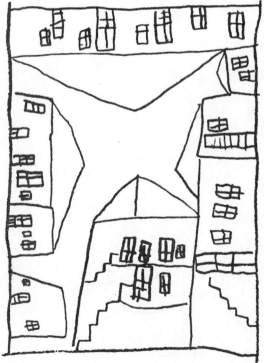

FIG. 38.—11 ; 7. D.
H. Street going
round a block
of houses.
Houses 'fold-
ed over' in-
wards.

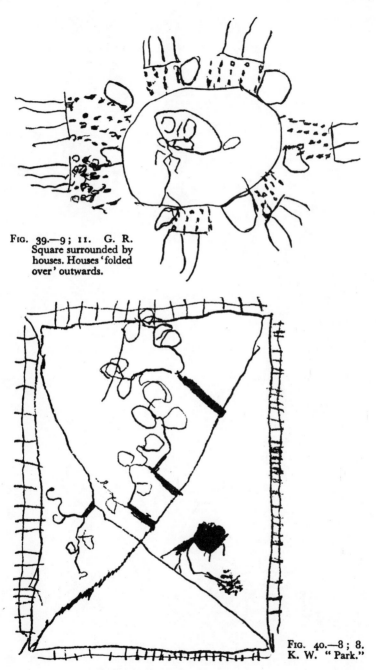

Fig. 39.—9; 11. G. R. Square surrounded by houses. Houses 'folded over' outwards.

Fig. 40.—8; 8. K. W. "Park."

FIG. 41.—11 ; 7. L. B. " Climbing a Mountain." Introduction of a symbol for ' mountain '.

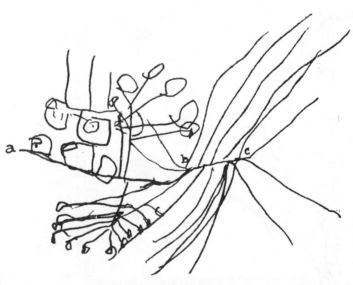

FIG. 42.—9 ; 11. G. R. " House on the Mountain." The mountain is given contour lines to indicate the steepness.

FIG. 43.—8 ; 9. D. H. " Mountain." Schematic association of the symbol for mountain with the base line.

FIG. 44.—8 ; 10. K. W. " Landscape." Importance of the base line.

Fig. 46.—12; 3. D. H. " Climbers Reaching a Hut."
Mixture of plan and elevation.

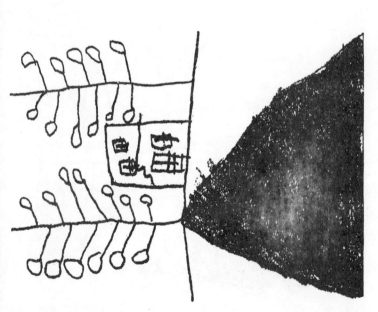

Fig. 45.—12; 1. D. H. " House on the Mountain."
Separate symbols for ' mountain '. Symbolic association of the house with the mountain top.

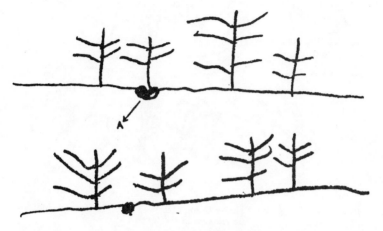

Fig. 47.—11 ; 6. L. B. " Street Going Over a Hillock." Introduction of a symbol without any relation to visual reality.

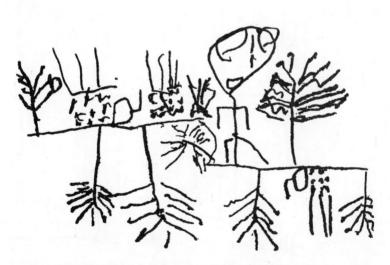

Fig. 48.—10 ; 5. G. R. " Street Going Over a Hill." Introduction of a symbol having reference to sensory experience.

FIG. 49.—9 ; 2. K. W. " Street Going Over a Hill." The base line indicates the changes in the terrain.

(d) *Subjective Space*

FIG. 50.—11 ; 5. D. H. " Dormitory." The subjective relationship to the object portrayed determines a totally different mode of drawing. Plan and elevation alternate according to the type of subjective experience.

FIG. 51.—9 ; I. K. W. " A Mine." Typical ' X-ray picture '.

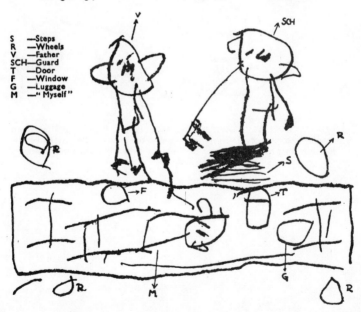

S —Steps
R —Wheels
V —Father
SCH —Guard
T —Door
F —Window
G —Luggage
M —" Myself "

FIG. 52.—13 ; II. A. B. " Saying Good-bye." In drawings, a mixture of plan and elevation, if introduced for subjective reasons, can also express movement.

FIG. 53.—8 ; 8. K. W. " Excursion to a Mountain." ' Emphasised' and 'unemphasised ' space. Turning the plane of the drawing becomes a symbol
for movement. Significance of ' folding over ' in subjective space.

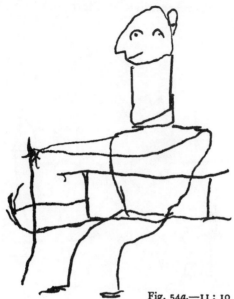

Fig. 54*a*.—11 ; 10

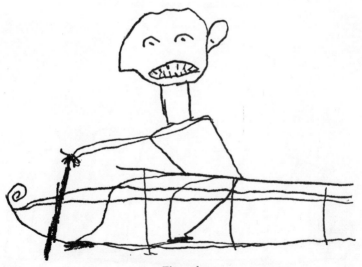

Fig. 54*b*

Fig. 54*a*, *b*.—D. H. "Sleighs." Bodily experiences determine the order relations in the drawing.

FIG. 55.—9. K. W. " Departure for the Summer Holidays." Representation of temporal sequences in single drawing.

FIG. 56.—11 ; 7. D. H. " Football Players." Representation of a sequence of motions in a single figure.

Fig. 57.—8 ; 8. K. W. " K Shakes a Nut Tree."

Fig. 58.—11 ; 9. D. H. " D Gets into the Bath." Repeated representation of the same person carrying out different actions.

O

186

Fig. 59.—11; 10. D. H. "D Sneezes, Blows his Nose, and puts the Handkerchief in his Pocket." Different movements represented in a single figure.

Fig. 60.—11; 9. D. H. "D bids Farewell to his Father." Numerous symbols and experiences put together in a single picture.

FIG. 61a.—8 ; 8. K.W. Streetsinger.

FIG. 61b.—8 ; 7. K.W. Someone calling someone else.

FIG. 61c.—8 ; 9. K. W. Someone coughing. Representation of sound and noises in a drawing.

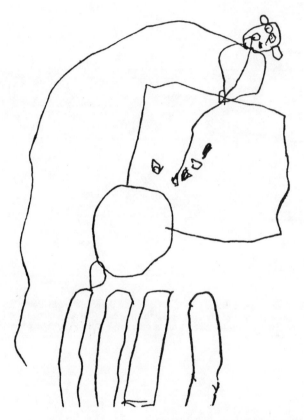

Fig. 62.—(4½ years). " Elephant eating Sugar." Non-visual symbolic representation.

Fig. 63. See page 193.

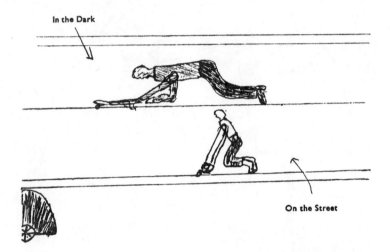

In the Dark

On the Street

Fig. 64.—" Someone loses a Coin, first in a Dark and then in a Light Place."
The consciousness of self in dark and light places. (These illustrations
are characteristic examples taken from a very large number treating the
same topic.)

Fig. 65 (7 years). "You are Shown Your Presents." Expressive Over-emphases. (Again one of innumerable characteristic examples.)

FIG. 66 (5 years). "A Girl Sees a Flower, Picks It and Puts It in the Basket."
Simultaneous representation of different phases of time. The first sight
of the flower gives rise to an experience and the flower is drawn very
large and in detail. When the girl has picked the flower, it becomes
simply one among many in the basket, is undifferentiated and treated
casually.

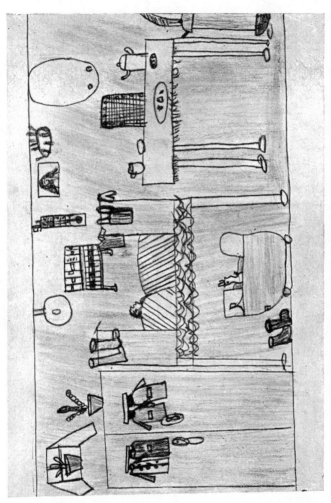

FIG. 63. (7 years.) "Bedroom." Use of baseline; subjective and objective space.

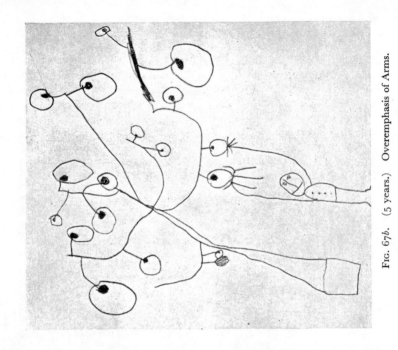

Fig. 67b. (5 years.) Overemphasis of Arms.

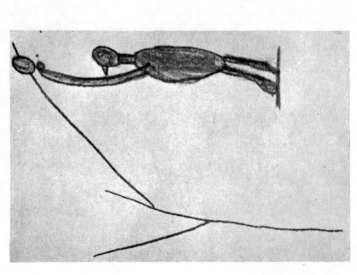

Fig. 67a. (5 years.) Inflexible Tree Schema.

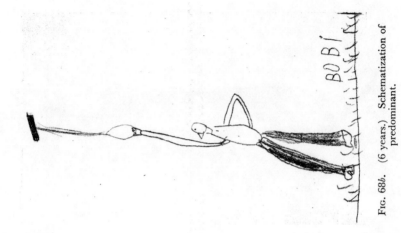

Fig. 68a. (6 years.) Overemphasis of human figure to indicate stretching.

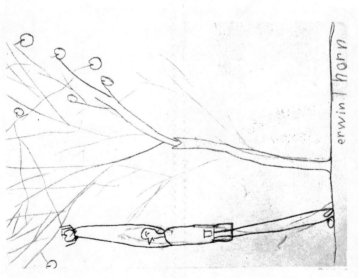

Fig. 68b. (6 years.) Schematization of predominant.

FIG. 69b. (7 years.) Overemphasis of body length.

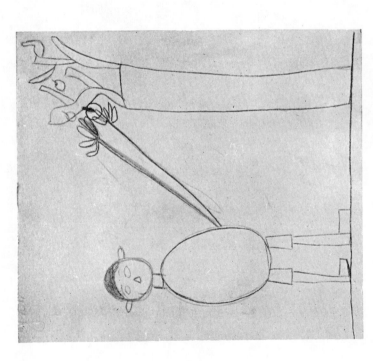

FIG. 69a. (7 years.) Overemphases still predominate in representing the human figure.

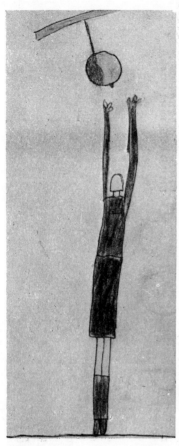

Fig. 70a. (8 years.) The importance of the apple is emphasized. Number of human and tree schemata approximately equal.

Fig. 70b. (8 years.) Frequently no relation can be established between figure and tree.

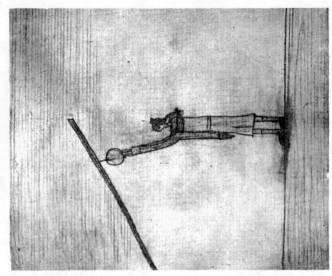

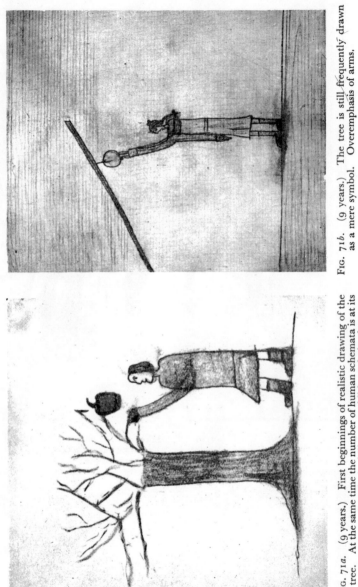

Fig. 71a. (9 years.) First beginnings of realistic drawing of the tree. At the same time the number of human schemata is at its maximum as well as the inability to establish a relation between tree and figure.

Fig. 71b. (9 years.) The tree is still frequently drawn as a mere symbol. Overemphasis of arms.

Fig. 72a. (10 years.) Naturalistic drawing begins.

Fig. 72b. (10 years.) The apple is especially emphasized. There is still a frequent lack of relation between tree and figure.

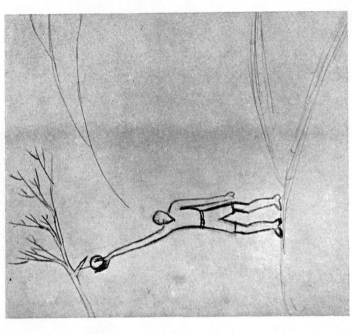

FIG. 73a. (11 years.) Rapid increase of realistic drawings of trees. Disappearance of the inflexible schema. Overemphasis of the tree.

FIG. 73b. (11 years.) Overemphasis of the arm and the grasping hand.

Fig. 74a. (12 years.) Increase of realistic drawings. Overemphasis of tree.

Fig. 74b. (12 years.) Increase of realistic drawing.

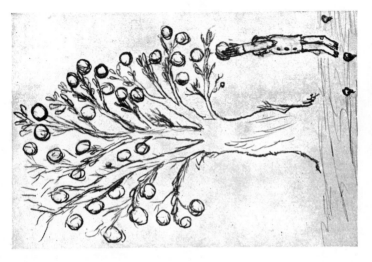

Fig. 75b. (13 years.) Overemphasis of apples and grasping hands.

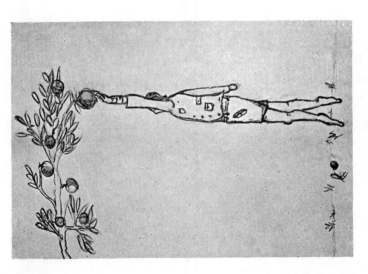

Fig. 75a. (13 years.) Realistic drawings predominate and details are shown.

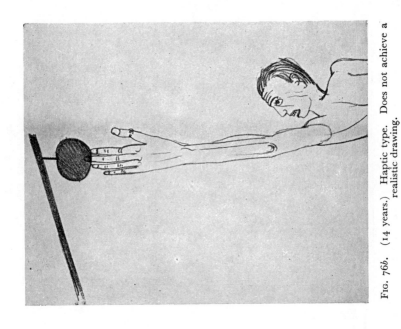

Fig. 76a. (14 years.) Realistic drawings with greater emphasis on the human figure.

Fig. 76b. (14 years.) Haptic type. Does not achieve a realistic drawing.

PLATES

Where numbers follow the Plate number, they give the age of the pupil in years and months. Where no initials are given the pupil is normal sighted.

PLATE 1. (13 years.) "Moses Strikes the Rock that Water May Flow."
Normal sighted ; visual type.

PLATE 2. (13 years.) As above. Haptic type.

PLATE 3. (13 years.)
" Jacob's Dream."
Normal sighted ;
visual type.

PLATE 4. (13 years.) As above. Haptic type.

PLATE 5b. (16 years.) M. B. Drowning Man. (Detail from "Egyptians drowning in the Red Sea.")

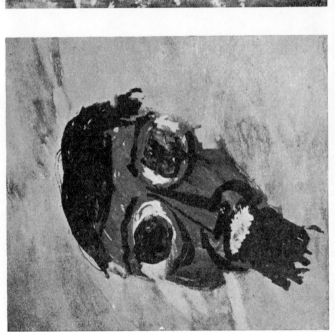

PLATE 5a. (12 years.) Sch. G. "Drowning Man."

PLATE 6. (13 years.) " The Deluge." Normal sighted ; haptic type.

PLATE 7. (13 years.) " Moses Breaks the Tablets." Normal sighted ;
haptic type.

PLATE 8. (23 years.) J.M. "Being Throttled." The powerful sensations concentrated in the eyes are represented by much exaggerated bulging eyeballs. Weak sighted ; haptic type.

PLATE 9. (18 years.) Blind. "Longing for Sight." Congenitally blind ;
visual type.

PLATE 10*a*. (13 years.) S. Gr. " Street."

PLATE 10*b*. (13 years.) S. Gr. " School on Fire."

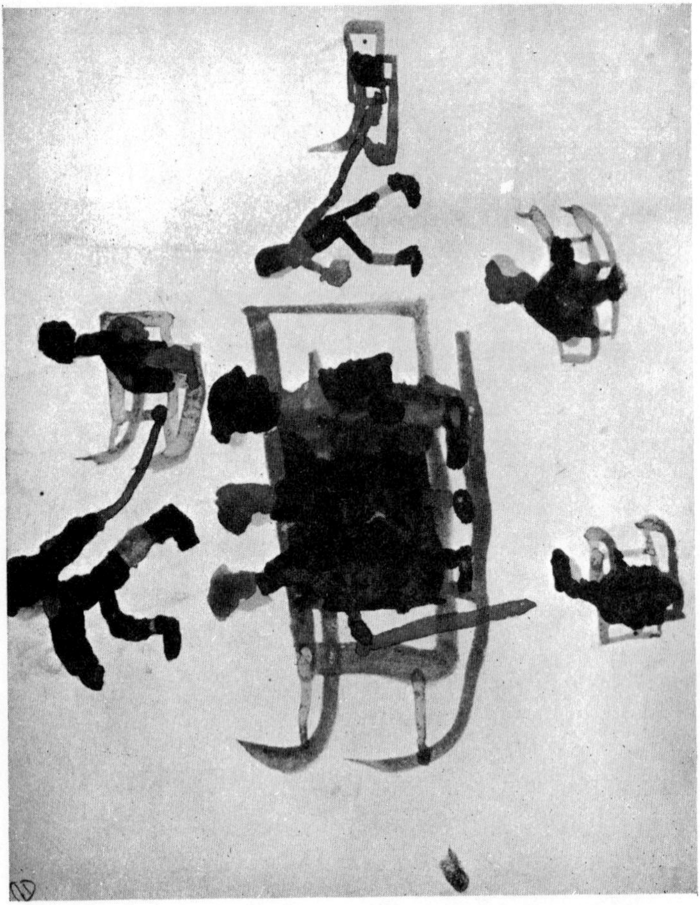

PLATE II. (14 years.) S. Gr. "Sleighs."

214

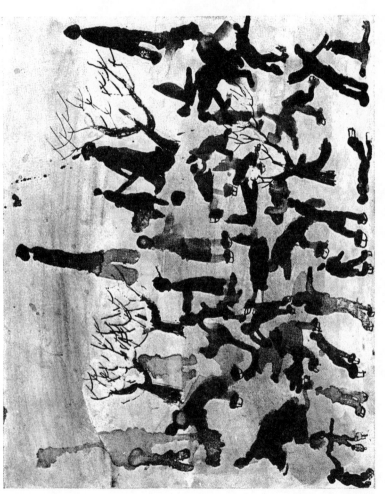

PLATE 12   (14 years.)   S.Gr.   "Skaters on the Ice"

PLATE 13a.   (15 years.)   M. B.   " Forest under Snow and Woman Gathering Wood."

PLATE 13b. (13 years.) S. Gr. "Forest under Snow and Woman Gathering Wood."

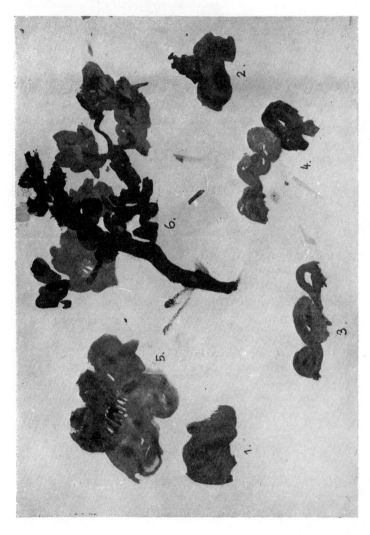

PLATE 14a. (12 years.) Sch. G. Spray of Flowers, drawn from nature.

PLATE 14*b*. (12 years.) Sch. G. Spray of Flowers, drawn from memory.

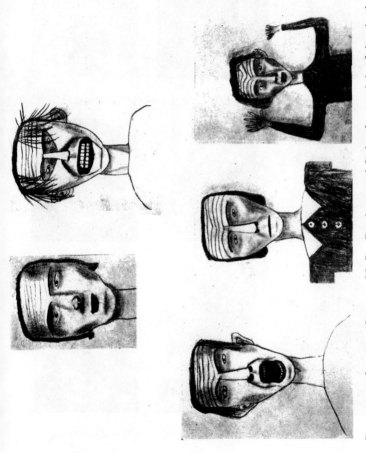

PLATE 15. 18 ; 4 to 18 ; 10. M. B. Developmental Series characteristic of the visual type. (1) Proletarian Woman, (2) Angry Man, (3) Screaming Man, (4) Exalted Woman, (5) Fanatical Orator.

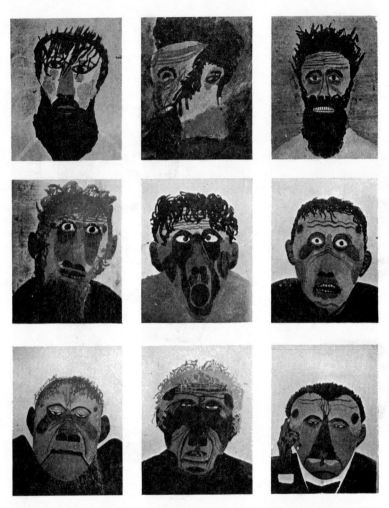

PLATE 16.   15 ; 4 to 16 ; o.   H. A.   Development Series characteristic of the
haptic type.

PLATE 18.   15 ; 5.   H. A.   "Laughing Man."

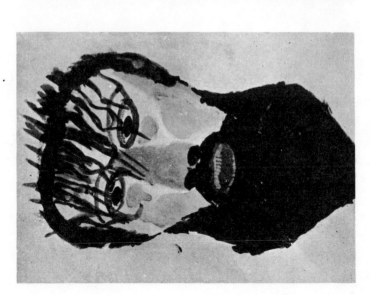

PLATE 17.   15 ; 4.   H. A.   "Drowning Man."

PLATE 20. 16 ; 0. H. A. " Beggar."

PLATE 19. 15 ; 6. H. A. " Angry Man."

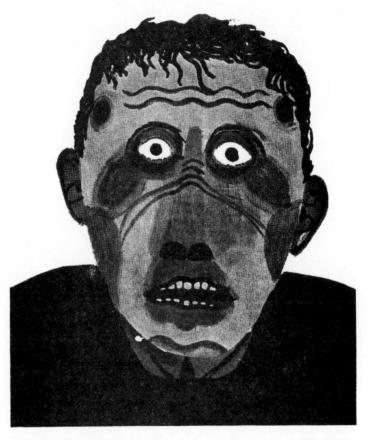

PLATE 23. (15 years 9 months.) H.A. "Man Trembling with Fear"

[face p. 223

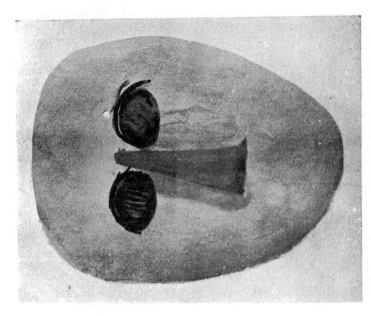

PLATE. 22. 15 ; 9. H.A. Incomplete drawing. This is an intermediate stage of the mask " Man Trembling with Fear ", Pl. 23.

PLATE 21. 15 ; 7. H.A. " The Cry for Help."

PLATE 24. 15 ; 9. H. A. "A Father Hears of the Death of His Son."

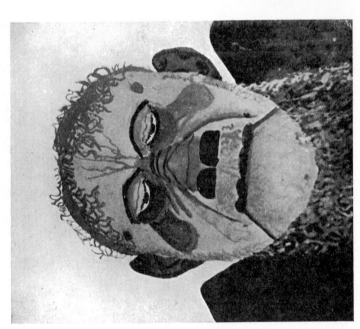

PLATE 25. 15 ; 11. H. A. "Exhausted Proletarian Woman."

PLATE 27. (17 years.) S.Gr. "Sunset"

[face p. 225

Plate 28.   18 ; o.   G. St.   " Angry Man."

Plate 26.   16 ; o.   H. A.   " Chess Player."

225

PLATE 29. (Blind.) "Listener." Congenitally blind; haptic type. Reproduced from Ludwig Münz and Viktor Lowenfeld, *Plastiche Arbeiten Blinder.* Rohrer, Brünn, 1934. Photograph by L. Münz.

PLATE 30. 17 ; 0. G.St. " Listener."

PLATE 31b. 19 ; 0. G.St. "Officer."

PLATE 31a. 19 ; 0. G. St. "Moses Hears the Jews Dancing Round the Golden Calf."

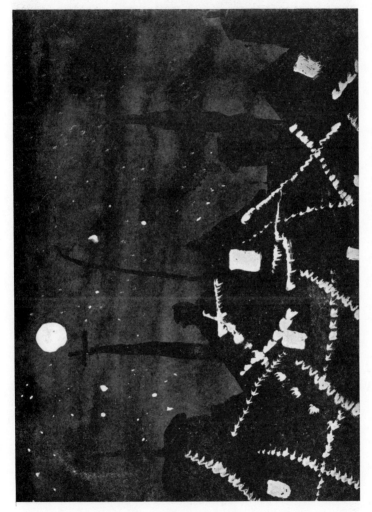

PLATE 32. (14 years.) S. Gr. "Town by Night."

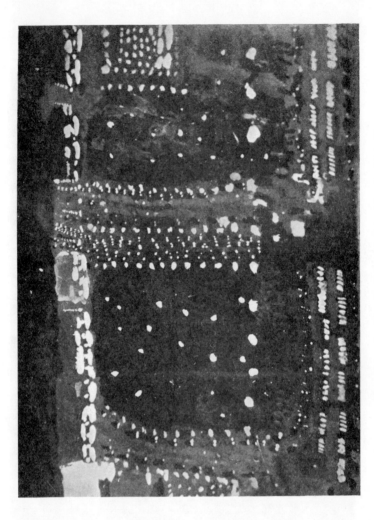

PLATE 33. (14 years.) Sch. G. "Accident by Night."

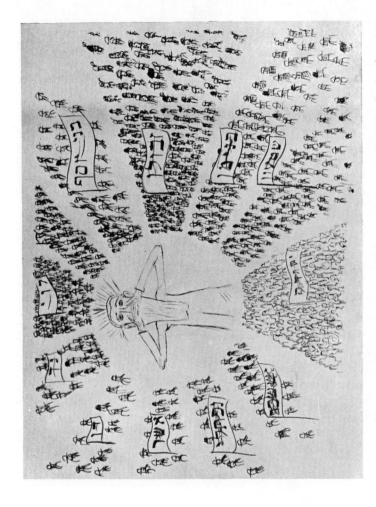

PLATE 34. (14 years.) "Moses Bids Farewell to his People." Normal sighted; haptic type.

PLATE 35. (17 years.) (Blind.) "Youth Imploring." Congenitally Blind.

PLATE 36. (16 years.) S. Gr. " Woman Gathering Wood."

PLATE 38.   (12 years.)   Sch. G.   "Orator."

PLATE 37.   (14 years.)   Sch. G.   "Attack on a Public Building."

234

PLATE 39. (16 years.) S.Gr. A Beggar Goes Over the Street, is Knocked Down by a Car, and Loses Hat and Money.

PLATE 40. (14 years.) Sch. G. "Fire."

236

PLATE 41. (18 years.) M. B. " Proletarian Woman Grieves for Her Child."

PLATE 43. (17 years.) M. B. "Street Singer."

PLATE 42. (18 years.) M. B. "Street Singer."

PLATE 45. (19 years.) M. B. "Faded Woman."

PLATE 44. (18 years.) M. B. "Thinker."

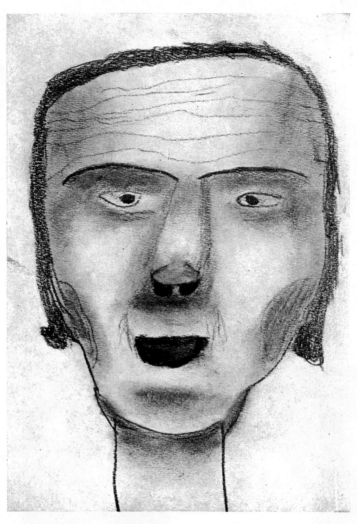

PLATE 46. (19 years.) M. B. " Proletarian Woman."

PLATE 47.   (19 years.)   M. B.   "Angry Man."

PLATE 48. (19 years.) M. B. " Man Screaming."

PLATE 49. (19 years.) M. B. "Fanatical Orator."

PLATE 50.   (13 years.)   Sch. G.   " Beggar and Child."

PLATE 51. (15 years.) Sch.G. "Street Scene"

[face p. 244

PLATE 52. (20 years.) M. B. " Old Man by Candle Light."

PLATE 53a. (14 years.) S. Gr. "Swans On a Pond."

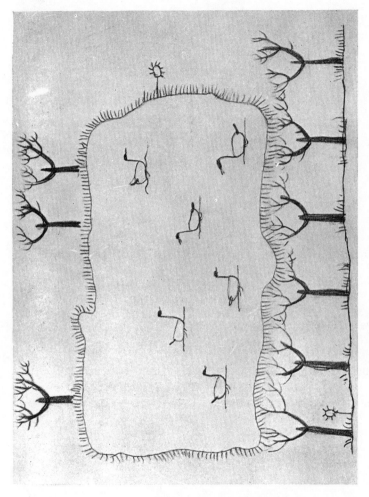

PLATE 53b. (14 years.) S. Gr. "Swans On a Pond."

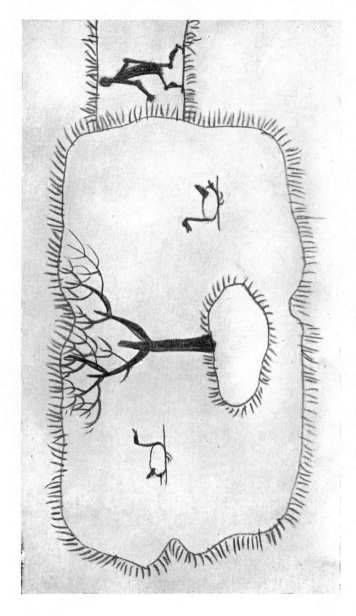

PLATE 54. (14 years.) . Gr. "Island with Tree."

PLATE 56.   (16 years.)   M. B.   " Orator."

PLATE 55.   (14 years.)   G. K.   " Orator."

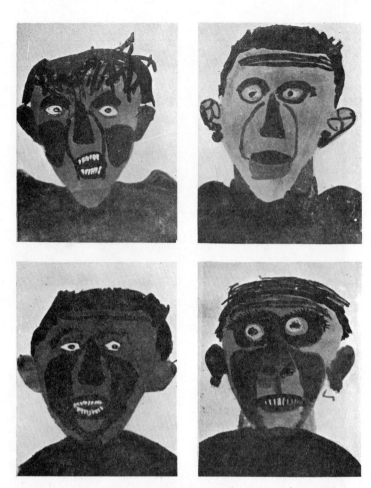

PLATE 57a.   Expressive masks that have remained stationary.   Haptic type.

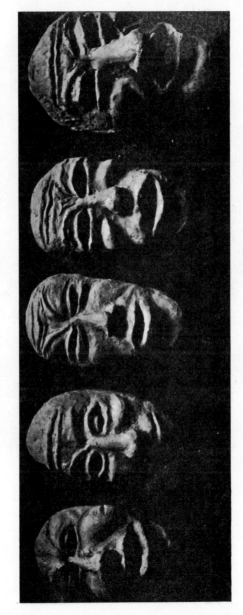

PLATE 57b. Expressive masks that have remained stationary. Inhibited haptic type.

PLATE 58.   (Blind.)   " Girl Weeping."   Congenitally blind, with only the most rudimentary sight.

PLATE 59. (Blind.) "Listener." Congenitally blind; haptic type. Reproduced from Münz-Löwenfeld, *Platische Arbeiten Blinder*. Photograph by L. Münz.

PLATE 60a. "Transport and Fishery on the Tigris." Assyrian Relief. From Otto Weber, *Assyriche Plastik*. Wasmuth, Berlin.

PLATE 60b. "Hunting for Birds in the Forest." From Otto Weber, *Assyrische Plastik*. Wasmuth, Berlin.

PLATE 61. "Hunting in the Desert." Detail from Heinrich Schäfer, *Von Ägyptischer Kunst*, Leipzig, 1919.

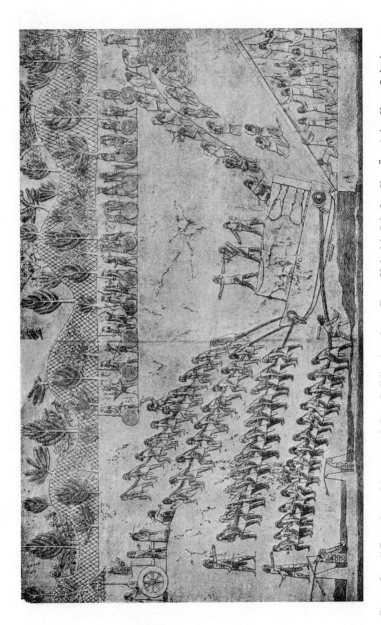

PLATE 62. " Dragging a Monumental Gate Bull." Assyrian. From Heinrich Schäfer, *Von Ägyptischer Kunst*, Leipzig, 1919.

PLATE 63a. Garden with Pond from which Water Carriers are
Fetching Water. Egyptian. From Heinrich Schäfer, *Von Ägyptischer
Kunst*, Leipzig, 1919.

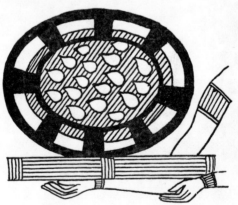

PLATE 63b. Basket and Contents. Egyptian.
From Heinrich Schäfer, *Von Ägyptischer Kunst*,
Leipzig, 1919.

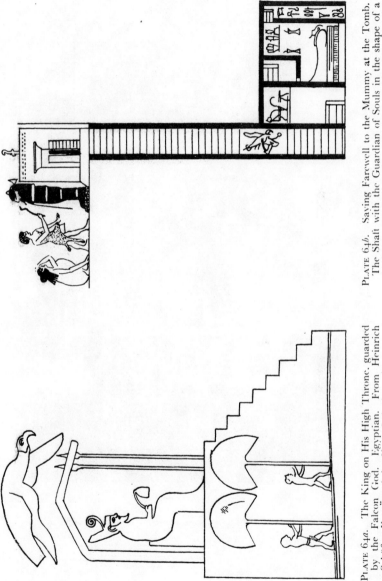

PLATE 64a. The King on His High Throne, guarded by the Falcon God. Egyptian. From Heinrich Schäfer, *Von Ägyptischer Kunst*, Leipzig, 1919.

PLATE 64b. Saying Farewell to the Mummy at the Tomb. The Shaft with the Guardian of Souls in the shape of a bird bringing food and drink, and the four subterranean chambers with the Mummy and the funeral gifts. Egyptian. From Heinrich Schäfer, *Von Ägyptischer Kunst*, Leipzig, 1919.

259

PLATE 65. From the *Sachsenspiegel*. (Heidelberg MS.)

PLATE 66.   Uli (ancestral mask) from New Mecklenburg, Bismarck Archipelago.   From Eckart von Sydow, *Ahnenkult und Ahnenbild der Naturʋölker*, Berlin, 1919.

PLATE 67.   Mask from New Guinea.   From Ernst Fuhrmann,
Neu-Guinea, Folkwang, Darmstadt.

PLATE 68. (Blind.) " Inner Decay." Sculpture by the congenitally blind P.H. ; haptic type.

PLATE 69. Head. Pacasmayo, Peru. From Ernst Fuhrmann, *Der Sinn im Gegenstand*, Munich, 1923.

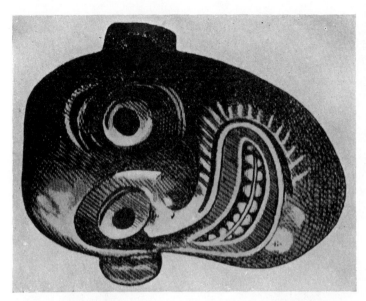

PLATE 71. Mask of the Devil with One-sided Facial Paralysis. Singhalese. From Max Verworn, *Ideoplastiche Kunst*, Jena, 1914.

PLATE 70. Head of the God Huchne-teo-te, Mexico.

PLATE 72. Figure (Wood). New Mecklenburg. From
Herbert Kühn, *die Kunst der Primitiven*, Munich, 1923.

PLATE 73. Adoration of the Magi. Ecbert Codex, Trèves, *circa* A.D. 990. From H. Ehl, *Buchmalerei des frühen Mittelalters*, Berlin, 1925.

267

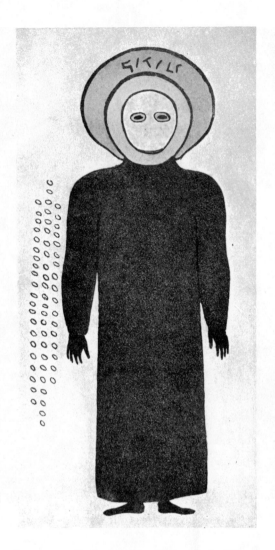

PLATE 74. Rock painting from North Western
Australia. From Herbert Kühn, *die Kunst der
Primitiven*, Munich, 1923.

PLATE 75a. Andrea Tafi, Apollonio Greco, *et al*. Mosaics in the Cupola of the Baptistery at Florence. Italian and Byzantine work of the thirteenth and first half of the fourteenth centuries.

PLATE 75b.   Rhenish work in the Romanesque style.   Gilded copper.   *Circa* A.D. 1130.   In the principal church of the former Benedictine foundation, Komburg.   Photograph by W. Kratt, Karlsruhe.

PLATE 76. (Weak sighted.) "Man Condemned to Death." Bust by a weak sighted haptic type. The psychic state of the man is expressed by the overemphasized sculpture of the muscles and hollows of the face.

PLATE 77. (Blind.) "Despair." Bust by a congenitally blind visual type.

271

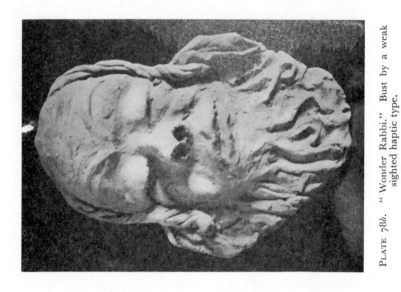

PLATE 78b. "Wonder Rabbi." Bust by a weak sighted haptic type.

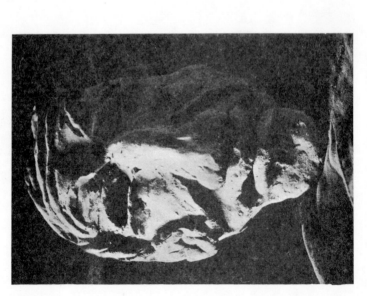

PLATE 78a. "Isaac." Bust by a weak sighted haptic type.